NOTES FROM A DAD MAN

Hilarious (true) tales of parenthood

Written By Ben Edge

CreateSpace Independent Publishing Platform

First Printing, 2016

ISBN 978-1541157460

"
This book is for pre-parents,
veteran parents,
grand parents,
Your parents
And ultimately my kids
And my wonderful girlfriend
(Who I love without measure) *"*

Contents

Prologue

YOU PROBABLY WOULDN'T think I was 30 years old. I've aged beyond recognition.

I look through pictures of myself before children and see a fresh-faced energetic young man with a sparkle in his eyes (Hope). The man I see in the mirror today looks more like a withered oak than something remotely resembling a man.

Sometimes I'll hold one of these pictures by the side of my face and compare the difference. It's almost like comparing spoiled fruit. If the young me is a ripe grape. The old me (the now me) looks like a bowl of porridge - these pictures are a snapshot of my life pre-children.

Children are exhausting on another level altogether.

My partner and I have a three year old daughter, Phoebe and a 6 month old boy, Zachary, who we love immensely. Before we had kids I had read tons of material describing the joys of parenthood, what I needed to do, how I needed to prepare myself and what to expect. It sounded challenging but ultimately doable. A bit like a 1000 piece jigsaw. Not out of my skill set completely, but a comfortable stretch that would culminate in something I could be proud of. Something I could stand back from, pat my partner on the shoulder and say 'Hey, we did it'.

I was wrong.

I have since discovered that everything I ever read regarding having children is a falsity, a sham and those that write that kind of stuff are nothing but charlatans. I presume they are written either by those who actually don't have children at all - in which case these books should really be labelled as fiction.

Or, I have a suspicion, these books are written by parents who know the real truth. Who look back on their Pre-child lives as I do and weep. Who see the young, healthy and stress free baby dreamers walking by and feel the pang of jealousy tug at the corners of their tired souls and think for a joke… Let's trick them into thinking having children is a breeze.

Perhaps it's a competition? These veteran parents gather together much like a witches coven, huddling round their laptops and thinking of ways in which they can make the future generation so woefully ill-prepared. They cackle as they type things like 'The first few weeks are the worst' and 'You'll quickly be wanting another'.

They're the type of parents who when speaking to their friends say, 'Oh, Jessica was a little angel' or 'Rufus had no trouble sleeping when he was a baby, don't worry yourself, you'll be fine.' And then they turn their backs with a smirk knowing full well Rufus was an absolute shit and there were times they genuinely wanted him adopted.

Don't get me wrong, you'll have good days - they do exist.

Oh the good days. Good days where everything runs smoothly, where your children are as sweet as a spring breeze, where all toys are packed away, all meals are eaten and you haven't stepped on a piece of Lego for the entire morning. Where being a parent seems effortless, like a gift from above and you go to sleep smiling and wondering why you ever worried about the what your child fed the neighbours cat the previous morning.

I, however, estimate that you'll get these moments once every 50-60 days. And there is certainly no recognisable pattern. I had to learn quickly that sometimes a good day will simply be a bad day disguised as a good one... Like a Trojan horse of exploding diarrhoea, temper tantrums, missing toys and ruined carpet.

The other days are more frequent. Parenting is like looking after a couple of suicidal maniacs who have injected adrenalin directly in their hearts. They're really just balls of heightened emotion with a penchant for bad ideas and repetition.

You'll be so tired that all you'll want to do is walk into the back garden, lie down on the lawn, turn into a crisp packet and float away on the wind.

I love my children more than I thought it was possible to love anything - that is the crux of why parenthood is so hard.

When you love something you want to protect it, nurture it, educate it, instil it with the sensibilities that as adults we take for granted (Fire burns and pouring water into the toaster doesn't create a cup of tea etc.). But children don't have these inhibitions.

What is a really bad idea to most functioning adults, is an invitation of challenge to a curious toddler.

And ultimately the most tiring part is that you become the villain. 'No Phoebe you can't stick the fork into the plug socket!' Cue; screams, wails, kicking, moaning and refusal to eat or drink for the entirety of the day - now you have a hunger strike on your hands.

Parents are heroes… There's no doubt about it.

It's just that instead of being seen as the Batman of the living room, your child will view you as the Penguin. That destroyer of light, good times and the final bastion of play dough.

It's a wonder anyone does it. Essentially you're ending your own life and resigning the next couple of decades to sleep deprivation, exhaustion, panic attacks and stopping little humanoids from settling themselves on fire.

I wasn't warned.

I read about changing diapers and warming milk bottles. And what to expect at certain points in my child's growth (e.g.. Walk, first word, liquid to solid etc.). But no where did I read the brutal realism of what raising a child was really like.

So I've written this. It's not a book you'll get any real lessons from. I'm not going to tell you how to change a nappy or get a screaming baby to sleep. What follows, is just a collection of experiences and illustrations of what it's like being a Dad to two children. There's no particular order to these stories - as my life is in no particular order anymore - it's a perpetual haze of 3am feeds, aggression and bouts of tears.

But it's real. It's basically a set of rambling notes from a mad(Dad) man.

So it begins...

Drawing

MY DAUGHTER IS CURRENTLY OBSESSED with cats, especially 'baby' cats. She makes me sit there and draw them by the thousand. Instead of drawing on her own and creating anything her imagination will allow, she forces me to sit down and churn out cat pictures like she's running some form of toddler sweat shop.

I have to draw the cats very small - otherwise 'they are NOT baby cats' - apparently. Once I've drawn a baby cat, I have to draw a slightly bigger one next to it and call it... 'mummy cat'.

I'm forced to draw them in every felt-tip and crayon colour she owns. The cats have to look happy. If I draw a cat which isn't the correct size or doesn't look happy enough then I have to start all over again as she rips the paper from my hand and throws it across the room. Why the fuck are these cats so happy?!… I ask myself as I draw my 780th cat of the afternoon.

Once she has a stack of paper with literally thousands of identical cat pictures, it either finishes and I'm free to go. Or if she's feeling particularly creative, the process starts again with a different animal, 'Now draw a baby Rhino'.

I'm an expert in drawing baby animals looking happy.

She then wants them plastered across the fridge.

I couldn't even tell you what colour our fridge is. It's covered top to bottom with shit pictures of ridiculously happy looking cats.

R.I.P Naptime

TODAY MARKS AN INCREDIBLY SAD TIME in our lives.

Nap times are no more.

That one hour period in the middle of the day when my daughter would nap; allow us opportunity to eat a slice of toast, scrub felt tip of the walls and extinguish fires - is no more.

It was glimmer of peace to look forward to… and it's gone.

If this wasn't heart-breaking enough on its own, it's had a knock on impact. Because she no longer naps she's so incredibly tired and grumpy by the evening that she's pretty much unbearable to be around between the hours of 5-8pm.

It also means a solid 12 hours of keeping her entertained, whilst simultaneously trying to keep the house from falling down or her deliberately trying to decapitate herself on the TV stand with no respite in between.

I may have to work alcohol more frequently into my daily routine as a coping strategy.

What's irritating is that she fights it so much.

She'll be lay on the floor; eyes red like she's just smoked 4 ounces of weed, screaming because her milk is too white or some other ridiculous reason. She'll then waltz about the house throwing things and randomly lashing out at inanimate objects.

Yesterday she kicked a chair and almost snapped her foot in half, then she threw herself on the floor and screamed for 2 hours.

It was so much fun.

The Jigsaw

I'VE BEEN AWAKE SINCE 5:30AM... It's evening now and I'm more tired than any human has ever been in the history of the world. The only thing keeping me going is the regular shots of caffeine I've been injecting between my toes.

Fortunately the kid's bedtime is on the horizon. By this point in the day you're basically just a bag of flesh with no ability to process thoughts. You have to summon your last ounce of energy to peel yourself from the couch to start the bedtime routine.

Tonight was different.

All of a sudden my daughter shuffles in clutching a large box. I know this box; I've seen it many times.

I stare down at her like she's walked in clutching the severed head of a fox. It's the 250 piece 'Frozen' jigsaw. 'Dad, I want to do a jigsaw before bed'. My life literally ended.

I've done this jigsaw before and it takes between 2-3 hours to make... It was clearly designed by someone who despises children. It's easily one of the most difficult and complex jigsaws ever created.

I tried to protest but she has that look in her eye. The look that says 'This. Is. Happening. Dad'.

I settle back down on the couch and hope that one of the jigsaw pieces is flung at my head at 150mph and kills me instantly.

After 2 hours we realise that 7 of the pieces are missing. I'm fuming. I look to see whether my daughter shares my feelings of outrage but she's fast asleep on the couch.

I pick up the jigsaw and burn it in the back garden.

Leaving the House

IF I LEAVE THE HOUSE on my own it takes between 2-3 minutes. If me and the girlfriend leave the house it takes between 1-2 hours. If me, my girlfriend and the two kids leave the house, it takes several years longer than the elephant gestation period.

I enjoy days out with the family, but I detest the stress, hassle and effort it takes to get everyone ready. My daughter is infuriatingly independent, meaning she has to get herself dressed no matter how long a process it is. So we're forced to stand around and watch her put on a pair of socks incorrectly 77 times, before mysteriously losing one of her shoes.

The other day she refused to leave the house unless she was wearing a straw hat - it was minus 5 degrees. My little lad is much easier to get ready as he generally just lies there. However being only a few weeks old he requires as much luggage as I'd take for a fortnight in the Malaysian rainforest. Bottles, wipes, nappies, formula, spare clothes, medication, blankets, dummies, rattles etc. etc...

You'll find that you'll only remember each of these items individually as you're about to leave forcing you all back inside, by which point my son has shit himself and my daughter has taken her tights off and is watching videos of some daft bint unwrapping kinder eggs on YouTube.

Ponytails

HOW DO YOU DO A PONYTAIL? The mind boggles.

My girlfriend is in charge of child aesthetics but the times she's not here I'm forced to try and replicate the precision, beauty and care that is required into doing a girl's hair.

I've tried to do it now about 60 times in a row and failed at every attempt. It's witchcraft. I'd find it easier to isolate a hydrogen atom. I've had YouTube tutorials up for the past 45 minutes trying to crack the case.

My daughter is growing increasingly more agitated. 'Dad, just hurry up and do it'. She's got more hair than fucking Rapunzel.

If I can't do it within the next 30 mins we aren't going out. If I take her out looking like this I'll be arrested immediately for child abuse and she'll be taken away by social services.

'If you can't do a ponytail Dad, just put it in plaits'. *She's taking the piss now.*

The Craft Set

THE 'CRAFT SET' is the name we give to a large bag of crap we keep on top of the fridge which contains several thousand of the worlds most irritating items; stickers, glitter, glue, beads, sequins, colourful card etc. etc.

It's a culmination of years of buying smaller craft sets, losing 80% of the contents within a few minutes and then bundling the rest into the big craft set box. We keep it hidden for our own sanity, and generally only allow it to come out a couple of times a year.

Even muttering the word '*craft set*' is punishable by naughty step. I'd rather my daughter play with a semi-automatic rifle than get the craft set out.

Typically when the craft set comes out within about 40 seconds the entire living is sticky, wet and covered in glitter that's impossible to remove. The couch is covered in sequins and there's beads glued to the TV remote.

She then gets bored after 4-5 minutes and swans off in the other room leaving me having to hire a crack team of industrial cleaners to pack everything away and pick glue out of the fireplace.

I absolutely loath the craft set.

Friday Nights

MID WEEK, LEADING UP TO 'DATE NIGHT', aka child free night, me and the girlfriend make elaborate plans that neither of us intend to go through with.

'Right, we'll get ready early, have a bottle of champagne, and just get the train to somewhere in Europe, and see where we end up. We'll just take our passports, a change of socks and £3000 in cash'.

Friday night rolls around… *'let's have a quick power nap first and recharge the old batteries - In fact - shall we order a takeout instead and watch that Documentary about penguins we've been itching to watch?'*

Nesting

SO PRETTY MUCH EVERY DAY over the past couple of weeks I've come home to find my girlfriend 'nesting'. Apparently women get a deep desire to perform home improvements just before the baby is born.

Today I came home to find my girlfriend, 8 months pregnant and the size of a Nissan Juke balanced precariously on a 9ft ladder painting the ceiling in the baby's room. I had to talk her down with the promise of chocolate and grapefruits.

I came home a few days ago and found she had started painting all the skirting boards in the house. Our house has about 15 miles of skirting boards - it's a job that would take around seven years to complete.

If I question the logic behind any of these tasks I'm liable to have my face bitten off. So I just have to grit my teeth and help out. I'm not sure our new-born baby is going to be overly upset that the roof hasn't been re-shingled.

I'm scared to leave in case I come home and find that she's smashing up the kitchen with a sledgehammer or trying to build a conservatory.

Get Me To Sleep

IMAGINE YOU'VE HAD 12 MINUTES REST in five days, you're seconds away from imploding and somebody hands you a giant bag of hamsters. Before you're allowed to sleep you have to *somehow* get the hamsters to stop wriggling. But... there's an interesting catch... The hamster's have been up all night doing crack cocaine and are... Completely. Fucking. Wired.

That's the struggle when your exhausted girlfriend thrusts a screaming newborn into your arms.

I've honestly walked the equivalent of Scotland and back tonight rocking Zachary to sleep. I've weaved a trench in the landing carpet.

He sleeps all day and then as night descends he discretely injects himself with caffeine. It's almost 10pm and I've not seen him blink for four hours.

I'm starting to think he's nocturnal - like a hedgehog.

I'm Going To Be A Dad

When I found out I was going to be a Dad I Initially felt an overwhelming mixture of emotions.

Part of me was so incredibly happy I wanted to snuff it right there and then to preserve the euphoric moment. Then there was another part of me that was hit with a sudden overwhelming dread. I realised that I was going to have responsibility over another human life. I was incapable of even looking after myself.

My Mum still booked doctors appointments for me, I couldn't cook anything more interesting than a pot noodle, I couldn't change a light bulb and every pet I'd ever owned had succumb to a tragic death. Like when I let my guinea pig out upstairs and it committed suicide by throwing himself off the bannister. Now I was going to be looking after an actual human baby.

I wanted to get in my car and drive to a remote fishing village in northern Scandinavia and live my life selling postcards. The reality is that you are much less prepared than you think you are. But you just sort of bundle along and wing it. It's a bit like being given the leading role in a play but nobody bothers to give you any lines or direction. Then the play starts and somebody thrusts a screaming child at you and says 'action'.

The first year with my daughter is an utter blur to me now; the sleepless nights, the constant feeling of drowning in a sea of despair had been eradicated from my memory.

I think it's nature's subtle trick to get you to do it again.

When I found out I was having another child I was again very happy. Two kids is perfect, and having a newborn is easy I told myself. However over the past few weeks my mind has been slowly picking up snippets of memories from the first time around and I'm gradually become terrified again.

I've forgotten everything I learnt the first time. I'm slowly remembering the feeling of extreme exhaustion, and having to boil the kettle 15 times a night. I've forgotten how to change a nappy, but I'm remembering more than a few occasions where I screamed into a pillow.

I have no affinity to god or religion but I also remember brushing my teeth in the bathroom with tears in my eyes praying that my child slept for longer than 2 hours.

The Arguments

Me and the Mrs have our fair share of silly disagreements and petty arguments as most couples do. But there is nothing quite as ridiculous as the arguments we have at 3am when the baby needs feeding.

I almost moved back in with my Mum last night because my girlfriend called me a knob head for not leaving the bibs on the side. I was shouting at her as she was taking too long to prep the bottle and she screamed at me for not winding him for long enough calling me - 'useless....'

In my sleep deprived mind, I misinterpreted this. *'Oh I'm a shit Dad now then am I!? Maybe you should go find a new partner then!'* In the end we both told each other to fuck off.

I stormed downstairs to sleep on the couch. The heating hadn't been on laying on a leather couch felt colder than Serbia at Xmas.

As I lay there literally shivering to death with no covers feeling like Kate Winslet from Titanic on the wooden door, I thought how stupid our argument was. I went back upstairs and got back in bed. We both apologised to each other and said how silly it was and that we loved each other etc. etc.

This happens every night.

Trip

Well we took our first trip out today as a foursome. It took 5 hours to get everything prepared and packed but we made it all the way to the zoo.

Having unloaded everything out of the car we realised we'd forgotten to bring our new-borns pram. So for the entire trip around the zoo I was forced to carry my son around in his car seat like a massive dumbbell. Despite weighing only 10 pounds himself - the car seat weighs a hefty 300 pounds and after 30 mins of walking him around in his not-so-mobile chair he felt like he weighed 19 stone. My arms were almost falling off by the time we sat down to have lunch. We then realised we'd forgotten the *'red bag'*, which contains all his milk, formula, nappies and bibs.

Keen for our new born to not starve to death we had to cut the trip short. My daughter was less than impressed at us having to leave and threw herself on the floor and wailed like a banshee. I had to carry my son 'the cannon-ball' in one hand and fireman's carry my daughter, who was screaming and punching me in the side of the head all the way back to the car.

We've decided we are doing no more trips until the kids both turn 18.

Sun Cream

WHENEVER THERE IS AN OUNCE OF SUNSHINE in the sky my girlfriend assumes the temperature is 58 degrees and that the UV from the sun is strong enough to strip paint. So she puts factor 15,000 on the kids in such depth she looks like she's shovelling cement over them.

This means my kids are the whitest children that have ever lived. In certain lights, my daughter is actually transparent. I don't actually think my son has felt any direct sunlight on his body since he was born. She then ensures that they spend their entire time hidden in the shade or wearing a hat the size of a gazebo.

They're not fucking gremlins - they will not react and reproduce when touched by direct sunlight. When we're out, if I'm holding my daughter's hand, I look like I'm walking along with a large bottle of semi-skimmed milk.

After our recent holiday the kids managed to come back whiter than when they left. My son looked like he'd been painted eggshell white.

Xmas List

MY DAUGHTERS CHRISTMAS LIST is basically just every advert she has seen on TV in the last three months. There isn't a product in the universe that she doesn't want. After every advert she says, '*can I have that for Xmas?*'....

'*But Phoebe that's an ab roller*'...

Her Christmas list currently ranges from a talking panda to a travel iron and a whisk.

Rain Man

My daughter has developed a Rain Man like memory to the point where she could probably, in detail, describe her own birth. She's also at an extremely volatile age where she goes from sweet to full blown tantrum in under 0.1 seconds.

The other day she asked me whether Ballou from 'The Jungle Book', was a girl or boy... I said boy. She swan dived into the rug and screamed until I swore it was a girl (she has this thing where everything has to be a girl). This is the type of personality we're dealing with at the moment.

She bought a cornflake cake home from nursery about a week ago and didn't want it so it went to the back of the fridge. This evening I fancied something sweet, and found this little cake hiding at the back. It was the only sweet thing in the entire house and I'd forgotten it was even there so I was made up. I chucked it in my mouth and despite it being a week old it was bloody delicious. I went back into the living room and thought nothing more of it.

Only 20 mins later Phoebe looks at me like a socio-path, deep into my soul and says, '*I want my cornflake cake*'. I felt my brain begin to melt.

My mind was scrambling for any excuse to avoid an epic meltdown. I came up with this...

'*Phoebe you are not going to believe what happened, Toby (her Nanna's dog) jumped through the window, opened the fridge and took your cake, I tried to stop him but he was too quick!!'*

It was a shit excuse I know, but I was crumbling by this point and my mind wasn't functioning correctly. Phoebe eyes my suspiciously then tells me '*We'll have to smack him later won't we?*'...I agree, sweat raining down my forehead - a solitary tear in my eye. She walks off content, for now.

I'm living with a beautiful psychopath.

Wet Doctors

I hate taking my son to the doctors on my own. He has this incredible ability to humiliate me every single time.

It also doesn't help that my doctor hates me. I don't know this for certain but every time she looks at me I get the feeling she wants me dead.

So today we arrive at the doctors and there we are sat in the waiting room. There's dozens of babies in there, and all of them are quiet and still - apart from mine. Mine is doing some form of robot dance whilst trying to jump from my hands and smash his head on the carpet. He's also making a high-pitched whistling sound without pausing for breath, the noise is so gut wrenchingly piercing my earlobes are melting off my face.

I try and smile but I look round knowing everyone in the room wants me dead as well. When the doctor finally calls me in, I bolt inside to escape the glares of irritated parents. Without making eye contact, I explain why I'm here. She looks irritated, like I've just asked her to pop round to mine and help me lay some laminate flooring. She asks me to strip him down as she leaves the room to fetch something… It's hot and I'm feeling anxious so I'm profusely sweating and my body is telling me to just run out the door. I take his nappy off and turn round to get a new one.

All of a sudden I felt warm liquid running down my back followed by a series of loud farts like machine gun fire. I turn to find Zachary forcing out a monster poo and pissing all over himself, me, the bed and the floor.

In terror I grab his nappy from underneath him to try and stop the outpour of urine. However in doing so, I ensured that I flung a dinner plate sized turd across the doctor's floor.

Cue doctor's entrance; there she finds me holding a soiled nappy, soaked to the bone with piss with her floor covered in several dozen shit pellets.

She'd honestly been out the room for about 45 seconds. We looked at each other for a lifetime. *'Kids hey'* I said finally, laughing awkwardly. She didn't even smile and I could tell she absolutely hated me and my child with every ounce of her soul.

She would have prescribed my son 3 tonnes of cocaine if it would get us out of her life.

Kids TV Shows

LAST NIGHT I SAT AND WATCHED 'In the Night Garden' with my daughter. She's obsessed with it, but I've never really give it much attention before today. It's probably the most haunting and disturbing TV programme ever made. The writers were clearly on some euphoric acid trip when they wrote it.

My daughter who is never still for more than 10 seconds is totally entranced by it. It was so bizarre that I found myself googling the hidden meaning behind the show whilst at work, suspecting that my daughter was actually being brainwashed into joining a cult.

She also likes 'Doc McStuffins' which is about a girl 'doctor' who fixes broken toys. It doesn't bother me AS much but it's not very realistic; she diagnosis toys with rare conditions such as Need A-Hug-I-Titis. It'd be more realistic if she diagnosed one of the broken toys with high blood pressure and type 2 diabetes. Either way the Disney channel is always on our TV from 6am until 8pm. Mainly it's just there as background noise, but you subconsciously pick up all the ridiculously irritating yet incredibly catchy songs. I had a Mickey Mouse song in my head for 3 days straight to the point I was honestly worried I'd never ever stop playing it in my mind, it nearly drove me to insanity.

Even when the kids are in bed and you're deflating on the couch it's still on.

After about an hour of my daughter being in bed asleep, my girlfriend looked at me and questioned why we were watching Paw Patrol. If you sit and actually watch these programmes you realise how fucking stupid some of them are. The plot holes in Paw Patrol alone are mind boggling.

A few weeks ago there was an episode of Curious George about germs that my daughter found absolutely hysterical. It wasn't at all. But for 4 straight days we watched this one episode over and over again until my brain was yelling at me to stick my head through the TV.

Too Cool

WELL AT 20 MONTHS OLD my daughter has apparently decided that's she too old and cool for lame formalities like calling me *Dad*, it's '*Ben*' now apparently.

I knew they grew up quickly but Jesus wept.

I caught her browsing Right Move earlier looking for a house to rent.

My daughter in the past few months has become a diva of monumental proportions. She looks at me now like I'm 'the help'. She only takes a bath if the temperature is 37.857 degrees and lightly sprinkled with honey, lavender and there's a harpist sat on the edge of the bath playing a selection of soothing anthems. Most kids her age enjoy chicken nuggets and chips etc. Phoebe has to have hand reared Argentinian beef, expertly prepared by a Michelin star chef, washed down with Vimto in a crystal studded beaker.

I get the feeling she looks at me and around her surroundings and thinks were peasants.

Party Bags

MY GIRLFRIEND LIKES to keep things interesting in the relationship.

I'm creeping out of the room at 6am this morning to go to work - she and the baby are asleep - or so I think… From under the cover of darkness she says 'Ben, while your at work, could you pick up 12 party bags for Phoebes party, 8 bottles of bubbles, 15 packs of pink sweets, 10 packs of white sweets and about 10 packs of kids stickers - thanks' Then she falls immediately back to sleep.

It took me the entire journey to work to rationalise this request and to try and understand since when in hell she thought I had quit my job and started working at Chuckles?

Gymnastics

SO MY DAUGHTER HAS STARTED gymnastics lessons. I've been able to take her this afternoon as I've had the day of work. It honestly makes me immensely proud to watch her having fun. However she's clearly inherited my distinct lack of grace and elegance - bless her. She moves like her joints are made of MDF.

The other girls in her class look like they've been doing gymnastics for 25 years and are future gold medallists, while my daughter jumps around like a thanksgiving turkey that's OD'd on Co-codamol.

I love that she has a hobby she actually enjoys. However it has it's drawbacks. She now insists on doing front-rolls in living room and rolls around like a hedgehog clattering into tables and the fireplace all evening. Then she tries to hop - she can't hop - and always ends up perilously close to falling and smashing her face on the TV unit. It's probably the 100th hobby we've tried to get her in to.

We tried swimming, but she picked up the habit of deliberately swallowing as much chlorine has her body would allow before throwing up in the pool and everyone having to jump out.

Then we tried tap dancing, but it was too loud - Ironic - given my daughter is loudest human that's ever lived

Then we tried ballet, but she would only go in the

room if I was stood in the corner and she was allowed to stay within a 1 foot radius of me. Meaning I was the only parent stood in the corner of a ballet class with my daughter hiding behind my leg like a frightened ferret.

'What would you like to do?' I asked my daughter after the 6th attempt at ballet. *'Just stay at home I think'.*

Not an option.

We tried gymnastics.

The first class ended after 4 minutes after my daughter came out of the room and announced she needed a poo, refusing to go back in once she'd been. The second ended after 11 minutes, when she came out of the room and said she didn't feel well.

She made an instantaneous and miraculous recovery 3 seconds after having left the building.

The third time she stayed in for a full 6 minutes before saying she needed a poo (again). I think she holds her poo's in for use in emergency exit strategies.

The fourth time though, she stayed for the full hour and loved it. We had found her hobby.

If this failed we were going to try either fencing or archery.

Stalling For Time

MY DAUGHTER'S BEDTIMES are getting progressively more complicated and drawn out. She won't go to sleep now until you've read her at least 7 stories, each one longer than a Stephen King novel.

I've had to resort to reading just the first line of every page as I don't fancy the idea of spending the next 5 hours reading a 30,000 word epic about a princess losing a fucking tiara.

Then she needs the toilet, *but not really*, which is always fun. Then she wants a drink of water, but not in the cup I've just bought up. She wants the one that's currently doing the rounds in the dishwasher. Then she wants '*Snuffles*'... Snuffles is a stuffed turtle she's not even seen in 22 months that's currently collecting cobwebs in the attic, but she *desperately* has to have it in bed with her tonight.

Then she says goodnight.

A three year old hasn't really said goodnight unless they've said it at least 134 times. By the time it's over I'm dead. Me and my girlfriend play spin the bottle to decide who has to go through this monstrosity of a routine as it's absolutely exhausting.

It took so long the other night that my girlfriend had grown a beard by the time she'd come back downstairs.

Neil Buchanan

MY DAUGHTER THINKS her Dad is Neil Buchanan. Her creative demands are becoming increasingly more elaborate.

It started off with simple tasks, '*Dad, can you draw me a pony*'. This has gradually escalated to the point she's now asking me to draw '*King Kong... riding a bike... in a skirt... looking happy... holding a kitten...*' She has no purpose for these pictures and they always end up in the bin. I feel like she's constantly testing me.

This evening I was asked to draw a '*baby lion in a long dress, riding a unicorn*', she handed me a battered yellow crayon and sat back and watched. My artistic skills are basic at best, but in my daughter's eyes I'm as gifted as Leonardo da Vinci.

By the time I had finished this picture, it looked like a cat dry-humping a large pigeon. She looked and me and told me it was '*rubbish*' and stormed off.

It was rubbish to be fair... but I know it won't stop her from coming up with some new impossibly elaborate creative assignment at some point in the (too near) future.

In my spare time I've been practising how to draw a variety of different animals so as not to completely embarrass myself when she fires me one of her ludicrous requests.

Three Meals A Day

THE THREE BASIC MEAL TIMES are breakfast, dinner and tea - unless you're a three year old, in which case you can also chuck in 17 '*snack and treat times*'.

The mornings start of with the same song and dance of me asking '*what would you like for breakfast?*' followed by the same predictable response, '*sweets*'... and so the game begins. After explaining why you can't have sweets for breakfast, and then running through every breakfast related item you possess in your home, you eventually compromise and serve your three year old two portions of sweets. Really though you have to put a bit of enthusiasm and cre- ativity into tricking them into thinking that whatever you are offering is completely out of this world amazing. '*Oh my lord! Look! We have these magical; Disney, frozen, Peppa pig raisins... and look! Oh my... see these magical, princess and fairy Weetabix!*'

After my daughter finally agrees to eat something sensible I'll set her up at the table and then the real fun commences. '*PLEASE eat your cereal*', '*It's too hot*', it's cereal and milk. '*PLEEASE eat your cereal*', '*I want to get a teddy first*' It takes her so long to actually start eating it that some- times the milk has evaporated. Eventually, after 45 mins and 2 and half spoonfuls of cereal, you give in and allow them to leave their desk as your daughter declares she '*isn't hungry*'. '*Can I have a treat*'? follows 30 seconds later and you're left with either being a terrible parent by allowing your child to eat a bag of milky way stars at 9am, or, you are forced to listen to the repetition of demanding sweets and throwing tantrums until lunch time.

I sometimes try and pretend I'm still in control by allowing early morning treats on the proviso that she at least eats some fruit first. After 3 blueberries, she's sat on the couch eating a family sized bag of Milkyway stars. I'm not sure who won.

She is constantly hungry... apart from at breakfast, dinner and tea. I made some chicken and pasta for tea last night and my daughter looked at it like I'd served her a sheep's head on a bed of anthrax. *'I don't like pasta!' she does. 'I hate chicken!' She doesn't.* She sat there with a face on her refusing to even lift her fork. There's very little in the universe as frustrating as a trying to get a toddler to eat something. I had to leave the room and compose myself more than once as I was at severe risk of driving her face into her plate. We battled for a further 30 mins, by which time the chicken had started to decompose. Then I tried an old and trusted trick... *'If you eat all your tea, you can have an ice lolly'.* She was like a dog eating hot chips after that little motivator. I even had to tell her to slow down at one point as she was cramming fistfuls of pasta into her mouth whilst trying to ingest chicken through her nose.

Toilet Training

'DAD, I'VE DONE A BIG POO IN MY NICKS!' She's literally stood 15cm from the potty.

My daughter is the least subtle human in existence when it comes to toilet etiquette. She's also just set the record for the longest time it's taken anyone to be potty trained.

We've been trying to potty train her for what feels like 18 months now and she just doesn't get it. We've tried everything. She's also not lying about them being big either. This one in particular was the like a giant fuzzy brown hamster.

'Keep her pants off in the house, that'll work' said one of our friends in yet another utterly useless piece of advice. For three days we tried this and we now need a new rug as she just walks around without a care in the world and just shits wherever she likes - like a cat.

I'm genuinely worried that she's going to be sat in a lecture at University in 18 years time in a pull-up and have the nickname *'pampers'*.

The Cat Masks

'RIGHT, PHOEBE. YOU'VE HAD A LONG DAY, and we've got a big day tomorrow. Its late now and I've read you 11 books and sang you the entire Disney Frozen soundtrack. It's time to go to sleep. No messing about now please, or getting out of bed I mean it'....

'Okay Goodnight Daddy' she says dreamily.

I turn off the lights and leave the room. About an hour or so later I go in to check on her. I open the door and its quiet (sometimes a good sign). So I turn the light on to check on her and almost have a cardiac arrest.

I look to find Phoebe, fast asleep, dressed as a fucking cat! She's obviously got out of bed and found a cat mask, complete with whiskers and ears. She'd also crammed her bed full of every teddy she has in her room - which is about 750.

I don't know what goes through this girls mind sometimes. I daren't disturb her, as I've not got the energy to start the bedtime routine again, so I tip toe out of the room leaving her to sleep looking like Mr Mistoffelees from 'Cats'.

Answering Back

IF I HEAR MY DAUGHTER say 'No' one more time I'm going to have to put her up for adoption or try and flog her on eBay.

She's three, and I feel like I'm living with a hormonal teenager.

I actually heard her say to my girlfriend earlier '*you are really starting to get on my nerves now Mum*', because she had asked her whether she was finished with her Cheerio's.

Yesterday I asked her to tidy her toys away, she rolled her eyes, '*tutted*' at me and then stormed out the room saying '*aaaarrgh, just leave me alone*'. The naughty step has her ass imprint weaved into the fabric she's spent so many hours on there now.

I'm hoping this is a phase but we said that 2 years ago so I think it's basically just her personality.

Haunting

HAVING A CHILD IS CHILLING AT TIMES. I thought my daughter was napping so I crept in her room and started putting some of her clothes in the drawers. It was dark and almost ludicrously quiet, too quiet. I turn around to leave and she's stood up in her cot glaring at me in absolute silence.

She had a cold, expressionless stare like a small sociopath. I almost leapt out of the window.

'Hi sweetie', I say, my words trembling as they leave my mouth. She continues to look directly into my soul and starts singing a song about a sheep very quietly. Then I'm changing her nappy and she's smiling sadistically and pointing at something near the ceiling.

I think she see's dead people. Or the house is possessed, either scenario is likely at this point but I'm scared of spending time alone with my daughter.

Teething

MY SON IS TEETHING. I assume he's teething, as for the past week he's been trying to eat his own hand. He shoves his entire fist in this mouth and gnaws at it like he's grown tired of having limbs and wants them removed immediately. He's dribbling so much I'm worried he's going to drown in a puddle of his own saliva.

I feel really sorry for him, as having had really bad tooth ache I can only imagine what it feels like having two bottom teeth trying to drive there way through your gums. But *holy shit* is he grumpy.

He's driving me absolutely insane at the moment. He whinges and cries continuously.

I'm genuinely trying to be sympathetic and have tried everything to sooth him, but after 7 continual hours of whining it's become difficult to not want to put him in the shed and go and grill my face on the George Foreman. I don't think I've ever wanted anything more than for these teeth to appear. He stopped whining for about 15 minutes earlier and I honestly thought I had gone deaf. He doesn't want to be held, or put down, or sleep, or eat.

The fact he's incapable of communicating in any other way than crying and whinging makes it so difficult to know what to do with him, despite me repeatedly pleading with him in tears to tell me what he wants.

I'd happily rip my own teeth out right now and sellotape them to his gums if it's just the teeth he wants. Apparently he will get 20 teeth by the time he's one. He currently has zero, with two coming through so it's going to be a long year.

It's hard to describe what a persistently crying baby does to your brain.

It melts it, until you feel like head is full of vegetable soup. These teeth must be like giant, razor-edged surf boards. I'd love it if babies were just born with a mouth full of teeth. They'd look fucking ridiculous granted, but it would save the sheer torture that is teething.

Odd Shoes

LAST NIGHT WAS ONE OF THOSE NIGHTS where you're on the way to work trying to calculate the number of minutes you actually slept. Was it 18 mins total sleep, or was it 24 mins TOTAL sleep?

Both kids were unwell, which meant settling one, before immediately rushing to the aid of the other. The night was a blur of shushing, Calpol, rocking and crying.

The tears were mainly mine.

When my alarm eventually went of at 5:30am, it felt like I'd been subjected to a prolonged and vicious assault before being left in a bush to defrost overnight.

When I looked at myself in the mirror it looked as though I had started to decompose. I lay in bed for 15 mins trying to formulate a plan to get out of work. I was even hoping I'd go downstairs to find we'd been burgled to just to get out of going. But alas, there was no decent reason I could come up with. So I crept down in the dark and got ready. I was so tired I fell asleep whilst putting my socks on.

Later at work I'm sat in a meeting struggling to focus on any words. I look down at my feet as eye contact is making me feel even sleepier. Then I look at my shoes and it takes me a minute or two to clock on what I am looking at.

I'm wearing odd fucking shoes.

In my weary state I've actually put on odd shoes.

Not even similar shoes.

One is back and square, the other brown and pointy. By this point it's 1pm so I've been in work for about 5 hours like this. Has nobody else noticed? I suddenly become hyper aware of my attire; it feels like my feet are size 27 and everyone within a 15 mile radius can see them. Odd socks are understandable. Odd shoes are absolutely unforgivable.

I feel like a hobo right now.

The Possessed Chair

THIS MORNING WHILST IN A MEETING at work my phone was continually buzzing in the pocket. After about the 8th time of doing it I excuse myself from the meeting as I assume it's important. I answer to hear my frantic girl-friend;

'Ben, we've got a ghost in the house!' She sounded genuinely terrified.

'What do you mean?'

'Phoebe's swing chair, it's in her room and it's going off on its own swinging back and forth'.

'It's probably just turned on because of a faulty battery or something'…

'No, it's that broken swing chair. Please come home and get rid of it!'.

I'm all for breaking free from work but it's difficult to rationalise leaving work because you've got a possessed swinging chair in the house. I told her to stop being ridicu-lous, and I finish the rest of the my day.

I arrived home later to an empty house. I ring my girlfriend and she tells me she's driven to her Mums house and is waiting there till I've got rid of the swing chair. I laughed and told her she was being stupid, but agree to go upstairs and remove it.

As I walk up the stairs I can hear it slowly creaking back and forth. I start to tingle and everything seems surreal and cold. As I peer my head into the room, I see it in the corner moving rhythmically. All of a sudden I'm frozen with fear.

I'm actually scared myself now because I know for a fact this chair is broken and doesn't have any batteries in it.

Maybe it is possessed.

At this point I can either go in and be a man and just throw this old chair out, or, we can go and live with my Uncle in Penzance and start a new life.

In the end I do the strangest thing. I start shouting really loudly like a hooligan and charge into the bedroom and kick the chair against the wall. I continue screaming as I pick it up and charge downstairs with it, run out into the garden, all the way to bottom and chuck it over my fence into the trees at the back.

After it's gone I look around struggling for breath. I feel like a bit of twat to be honest as I've just screamed the place down whilst clutching a swinging chair. I still have no idea why in the hell I did that. However... I did learn something important about myself that day... I'd be absolutely shit in a real emergency.

Bottles

SO IT'S NIGHT FIVE and breastfeeding isn't working. He cried and fed continuously from 6pm until about 3am. I rang the labour unit and asked whether I'd broken him, but apparently it was normal.

Part of me was hoping that they'd offer to come round and babysit while we went into the attic to sleep.

They suggested maybe trying a bottle to 'top him up'. We had formula, we had bottles, but we hadn't bothered to buy a steriliser. So after googling it, I realised I had to boil everything in a pan of water for 25 mins. So I ran downstairs in my undies, grabbed a pan out the cupboard and proceeded to boil a massive pan of water.

Water, I discovered, takes 700% longer to boil when you can hear the endless screeching of a child from upstairs and the intermittent sobs of an exhausted girlfriend.

Finally the water was boiling away and in went the bottles and teats. I watched the water bubbling away for 25 mins and it was hypnotic. I think I feel asleep with my eyes open leaning against the fridge….because I was aroused by a shout from upstairs *'Ben, where is the fucking bottle!'* I jumped up quickly and moved towards the pan, which was by now hotter than the surface of the sun. By the time I'd fished everything out I had third degree burns and my face was slowly melting like a candle. I then realised I'd forgot to boil the kettle, so had no water to put in the bottle. Meanwhile the screams were getting louder and I knew at any moment my girlfriend and or son were going to be thrown through the window onto the grass.

When the kettle boiled I filled the bottle, and carefully added the required scoops of formula milk. We were nearly there.

The problem now was If Zachary was to drink this milk; it would melt his internal organs as it was capable of dissolving glass.

I had to put water and ice in a bowl and let it cool down. This took another age and I learnt that our good friend water takes equally ridiculously long amounts of time to boil (from a pan), and to cool down.

When finally the bottle was ready, and the sun was creeping up I raced upstairs expecting to find Zachary locked in the sock draw and my girlfriend drinking a bottle of wine under the bed. But as I triumphantly entered the room, both girlfriend and baby were fast asleep.

'For fuck sake' I muttered before chucking the bottle on the side, and clambering into bed with half my body covered in blisters.

The Morning Ninja

I LEAVE FOR WORK EARLY, so I'm up before the sun comes up most of the time. In an attempt to ensure my girl-friend and the kids remain asleep and aren't woken by my getting ready I have developed the ability to sneak around like a ninja.

This means I've had to quickly evolve the ability to see in the dark.

Not unlike a bat, I can usually sense my surround-ings. However this morning having crept out of the bed-room and on to the landing I stepped on what I can only assume was broken shards of glass (it later turned out to be a plastic pony). I recoiled so much that I almost threw myself over the bannister. In agony and confident I'd need a tetanus shot I amble downstairs to get ready.

My kids are hypersensitive to sound so I have to get ready in the kitchen. In the winter months, this means try-ing to put your bill grundies on in temperatures so cold that even a polar bear would beg to wear a hat and scarf. Whilst getting ready once, I found a penguin frozen to death next to the sink.

It would genuinely be easy to go to bed fully clothed and then shimmy out the bedroom window each morning and brush my teeth in car.

Xmas Aftermath

I DESPERATELY NEED the universal price of cardboard to rise by 10,000%, so I can flog all three and a half tons of it I currently have in my back garden and be able to retire early and buy a modest Mediterranean island.

Each one of my daughters Xmas presents was wrapped inside 77 square feet of unnecessary cardboard. Our garden looks like a dumpsite with seagulls flapping around and families of cat sized rats playing hide and seek. I've got zero motivation to move any of it, as I've done nothing but eat Celebrations and cheese for the last 15 straight days and I'm now hideously fat and lethargic.

I'm hoping it either melts or evaporates. In addition I need somewhere I can purchase at least 205 packs of AA and AAA batteries on Christmas day, as each one of my daughter's toys kindly came with batteries not included and she wants to play every single one of them, all at once, immediately.

'Us' Time

IT'S BEEN ONE OF THOSE DAYS. The kids have been grumpy and we've battled relentlessly all day to keep them entertained to absolutely no avail. My daughter rolled her eyes at me that many times today that I threatened several hundred times to ring Santa. It's July.

To say we're looking forward to putting the kids to bed is a massive understatement. I even suggested putting the clocks forward by a couple of hours and pretending it's bed time so me and the Mrs can have a bit of quiet time. What's funny though is that we keep pretending to each other that we're definitely going to watch a film tonight and get a takeaway, maybe a couple of beers.

We both know that we're both lying.

About 15 mins after the kids go to bed one of us will say *'wow, it's been a long day'*, we'll then both yawn a few times for dramatic effect before conceding that we would both benefit from a good nights sleep, after which we'll trot of to bed and be asleep by 8pm.

It's nice sometimes to pretend that we have a normal life.

Impulsive Buyer

MY DAUGHTER HAS CLEARLY INHERITED my appalling desire to impulse buy.

Last week I purchased from Groupon, a 350 piece drill set (drill not included). I don't even own a drill, nor have any use for one, or know how to use one. Nor would my girlfriend allow me within 30 feet of one. So it's basically sat there like a big useless ornament. I bought it because it looked manly and shiny.

My daughter is the same. Every time we go shopping she'll pick up anything that catches her eye and asks for it. Yesterday in Morrison's she picked up, and desperately wanted to purchase; a pack of batteries, a red pepper, a copy of Heat magazine and a roasting dish. If I'm ever held at gunpoint in my home whilst the gunman demands 1000 small discarded bouncy balls, I'd be in luck. As behind my couch are limitless numbers of them. Each one represents an exhausting shopping trip where I've give in and bought her a bouncy ball.

Despite the fact that bouncy balls become 2 million percent less interesting once you get home. If I were able to find and successfully sell all the random crap I've purchased over the last 18 months, I'd be able to pay off the mortgage. Unfortunately there isn't much market for 30,000 half completed Kinder egg toys, or 15,000 part used sticker books.

Difficult Child

MY DAUGHTER IS GROWING increasingly independent and knows what she wants.

Obviously this is natural course of child development but it leads to me having several nervous breakdowns a day.

For example; she's discovered she likes sweets and lollipops, so getting her to eat anything else at the moment is near impossible. I'm there on my hands on knees screaming from the top of my lungs, *'please eat just a fish fucking finger!'* And she replies that she'll have a fruit pastel lolly instead. Or when I'm trying to get her dressed *'I'll wear my cat pyjamas', 'Phoebe, please it's 10am and you're going to nursery this afternoon'*, queue 45 mins of screaming….so Phoebe arrives at nursery wearing cat pyjamas and a straw hat eating a fruit pastel lolly.

When you've tidied the house and it finally looks like a house again and she comes over *'Get the glitter out'*… *'No Phoebe, let's sit here quietly and play with these spoons'. 'I want the glitter out'*….so 45 seconds later you're entire house looks like a gay grotto and there's sequins in the fridge.

I love my daughter but it's looking increasingly likely that she'll spend her entire teenage years grounded.

Washing Hair

WASHING THE HAIR OF A 2 YO'D is what I imagine it would be like to baptize a hysterical squirrel.

In her mind I'm actually pouring molten lava directly onto her scalp rather than warm soapy water. 'My eyes, my eyes they burn!' she cries before I've even put her in the bath. 'Tilt your head back' *hangs head over the side of the bath and screams*. Her hair is so thick and long that it's like trying to rinse a heavy carpet, it takes fucking forever to wash shampoo/conditioner out of it. By the time we're done, the water has started to ice over and her hands are more wrinkled than a ball bag. I wrap her in a towel and try and get her dry whilst she's screaming that she's cold directly into my face. I'm not allowed to use the hairdryer so I have to dry her hair with a towel.

Imagine trying to towel dry a massive mop that's absolutely drenched. I have to rub her head so hard and fast with the towel that there's always a high risk of starting a small forest fire. This takes even longer as every 15 seconds she'll jump out of my hands like a bar of soap and leg it around the house naked while I try and recapture her. Then she always wants the only pair of pyjamas that are in the washing machine, or, failing that she wants to wear a fancy dress outfit to bed.

So after several hours, she's washed, dried and ready for bed, dressed as a zebra.

Fickle Eating

MY DAUGHTER IS SO WILDLY INCONSISTENT with what foods she will and will not eat it makes any meal preparation impossible.

She changes her dietary criteria almost hourly. For example she went through a phase where she loved fish; salmon, sea bass, fish fingers, the lot. This made me happy as fish is obviously good for you and full of protein etc.

We had a three week period where she would actually ask for a salmon fillet for dinner. Then one day it stopped and mere mention of fish would make her fly of the handle and dive bomb into the carpet.

We've had this with lots of different foods; sausages, pizza, chicken, pasta, potatoes, cucumber. We're currently in a phase where she'll just about eat sausages and cucumber but only if the cucumber is cut so thin it's essentially slightly tacky water.

We've tried every vegetable that's available in Europe in an effort to stumble across something she'll enjoy. I've almost been in tears, pleading with her to eat just 'one fucking carrot' or to at least try 'a spoonful of peas' all while simultaneously trying to get her to sit down for longer than 4 seconds.

I've lost count of the times I've given up in a fit of rage and proclaimed that she 'can starve then', before 30 mins later realising that just like the Tamagotchi I failed to feed when I was younger, I need to get her to eat something or she'll die.

She does love parmesan cheese though, but not pasta at the moment. So she'll sit and eat a bowl of parmesan cheese the size of a Chinese takeaway with her hands. Parmesan cheese is fine on pasta but on it's own it tastes like your licking somebody's feet, so I have no idea how she finds any culinary merit in eating it...

The only food group she likes in it's entirety is sugar.

Before we hid the sweet cupboard in the garden, we once found her in the kitchen hunched next to the sink demolishing an entire family size bag of minstrels. She'd almost eaten the entire bag. Even I'd struggle with half a bag, and she had just essentially eaten 15,000 calories and 1.4 tons of sugar. She had a period of an hour when I genuinely thought her eyes were going to start spinning. She was running around in circles screaming, vibrating, and singing 'Let it go' like a crack addict. She then crashed out and slept for 2 hours before having a poo that was darker than midnight and weighed as much as a terraced house.

Value For Money

IF YOU SPEND ALL DAY AT HOME with a 3 YO diva and a new born, you start to become agitated like a caged bear.

By 9:11am my daughter has watched 7 films, painted, done every jigsaw in the house, taken every single one of her toys out, made glitter pictures and turned the house into Beirut.

She's been on the naughty step about 15 times by this point and I've been eyeing up the vodka for the last 45 minutes.

Supervising a three year old with no attention span is like having a dinner party with Zig and Zag. It's hard when there is just the one child but when you have a 2 month old who wants to cling to you like a Koala bear it's pretty much impossible. Essentially, the point is you need to get out of the house to break up the day and kill some time before you 'accidentally' stab yourself to death with a whisk.

I do actually enjoy taking the kids out but because the weather is so horrendously inclement you have to find indoor activities, which typically require the budget of a medium sized nation.

I went to the Aquarium yesterday. It cost around £60 to get us all in. After walking round relatively slowly, admiring each of the 7 fish they actually had In there, we reached the gift shop to discover we'd been in the aquarium, including a toilet break, about 15 minutes.

Even after going round a further 45 times to the point where even the fish were sick to death of seeing us we'd still managed only about an hour in there.

The gift shop was infinitely bigger than the aquarium and filled with the usual over priced pointless tat.

So after an hour we left with a dolphin bouncy ball and a small stingray pencil sharpener, both of which didn't last the drive home. I had spent the best part of £80.

It was 11:45am and still another 7+ hours till bed time.

Taking Charge

PHOEBE IS FINALLY STARTING to interact with her little brother - for the first three months of his life she just ignored him.

He'd be lay 4 inches from her screaming and she'd block him out like a negative thought. I think she was more than a little pissed off that we bought home a little brother for her rather than a little sister. When we told her she was having a brother she cried for about 3 weeks as she desperately wanted a sister.

I was secretly very pleased we were having a boy. As much as I love my daughter, she's aged me horribly. Plus it'd be nice to be capable of doing at least one of my children's hair without having a meltdown.

My daughter has now gradually come around to him though which was very sweet at first. But now I genuinely fear for his life. She now insists on being actively involved in everything from feeding him to winding him. That'd be fine, if she didn't hold him like a honey badger.

I came In the room before to find her trying to force feed him a Terry's chocolate orange. I then let her feed him and she rammed the bottle down his throat and almost knocked his gums clean out. She then told me he needed a nap, and she covered him in 79 blankets so after 3minutes his body temperature was hotter than the surface of Venus.

I'm trying to be encouraging as it's nice she's now

acknowledging his existence but I'm worried I'll find him in the oven because he was cold, or spinning around in the tumble dryer because he needed winding.

I let her help me change his bum the other day and she was so heavy handed that she almost decapitated his willy with a baby wipe.

Knowledgeable Friends

JUST IGNORE ANY ADVICE you get from friends or family when it come to kids.

When you haven't had a child before it's easy in your naïve and vulnerable state to be drawn into, and believe, literally anything that anyone tells you about what you need.

I quickly discovered on announcing we were having a child that all my friends and family were actually secret graduates from the University of raising children with a Masters degree in parenting.

Each had their own unique advice and opinions and each provided a gargantuan list of '*items we desperately needed*'. In retrospect, I should have ignored 99.8% of this advice. *We listened to all of it*, and our house quickly became Mother Care.

To this day we have items in the attic that make me incredibly angry when I look at them. Items we never used that we were convinced we needed or our child's head would roll off.

Within a few months we had about 2% of floor space available in our house, the rest was covered with jumparoors, walkabouts, play mats, breast pumps, milk heaters and mosses baskets and seventeen different car seats and prams.

Three months after finding out we were having a baby, my child, months from being born already owned more assets than me and my partner put together.

I had spent so much money by this point that there was a real possibility we'd have to sell the house and each live in one of the car seats in the woods. Basically if some-one tells you that you definitely need something, then assume you definitely don't need it.

Unfortunately all of this crap is impossible to sell because everyone else in the world has already been convinced to buy the same rubbish.

I've had a jumparoo on Gumtree for about 11 years and it's not even been looked at.

The Red Couch

BEING A PARENT TYPICALLY MEANS that after paying bills, buying food and spending money on your children for clothes, days out, toys etc. you're left with about £0.80p a week disposable income. I've often resorted to eating toothpaste at work for my dinners whilst the kids gorge on roasted guinea fowl.

It takes a lot for me to spend any money on myself. I once walked around with a pair of shoes with a 4 inch hole on the soles for two weeks before I finally decided to splurge, even then, only after I had stepped in a cold puddle and lost three toes to frostbite.

However we've recently treated ourselves to a new couch and Its bloody magnificent. It's like sitting on a cloud that's been woven with positive thought and happiness. It's my pride and joy and I love it only slightly less than I do my own children.

Yesterday however, my daughter was colouring on the floor and I was in the kitchen making her some lunch. I came back in to the room holding a sandwich and drink, and just froze... The sudden rage that filled me was so overwhelming I almost blacked out.

My daughter was drawing a fucking cat on the couch in red felt tip. Not just any cat, the biggest cat I've ever seen with whiskers 4 feet long.

I tried to shout but I was so angry the words

wouldn't even form in my mouth. I hurled the sandwich against the wall and made a high pitched gurgling sound.

Every felt tip in the house has now been destroyed and my daughter now lives on the naughty step where she will remain until her 11th birthday.

I tried for 3 hours to get the felt tip off to no avail. From this day forward I've decided we'll only furnish the house with polystyrene.

First Word

_____

FOR WEEKS WE'VE BEEN EXPECTING my daughter to say her first word. She's been rambling unintelligibly like an old drunk for ages now.

Today she finally said it.

However it wasn't the typical first word you'd expect, like 'Dada', or 'Mamma'. She said 'Cat'.

The word took us by surprise for sure. For one, we don't even have a cat... And I don't recall ever talking to her about cats. What *really* shocked us though, was that she said 'cat' in an deep Eastern European accent.It came out as 'sCATa'. And it's now all she says.

Very proud moment obviously... Although I'm more than a little concerned that my daughter has the voice of a communist shot putter.

Holiday

I LOVE RELAXING ON HOLIDAY. The one time you can forget all about work and responsibility. Unless of course you have kids.

Imagine being in a beautiful part of Portugal, waking up to the glorious sunshine and deciding to go for a swim in the pool. You pour yourself a beer - as you're on holiday so why not. You're enjoying the peace and serenity as the warm rays caress your soul and your drift across the pool like a Lili pad on a lake of clouds. It's so quiet you can hear the blood coursing through your veins. Then the silence is suddenly shattered.

'Aww Ben, Phoebe has just done a massive shit in the pool!'

I snap out of my daze to find Phoebe stood in the shallow end of the pool next to a turd the size of a crocodile.

She's screaming, as even she is utterly terrified at the size of this brown bungalow she's just released. I then spend the next hour chasing a poo around the pool with a bucket.

Nothing brings you back down to reality or emphasises the role of a Dad, then were you're treading water trying to chase down a shit

Arriving Home

AFTER A LONG DAY IN WORK where much of it was spent sleeping with my eyes open, I finally arrive back to the sanctuary that is home. I'm looking forward to kicking my shoes off and switching my brain off for the evening as I relax in the couch. As I put my keys in the door I suddenly remember... I have kids.

I gently open the front door and there's Phoebe, drinking red bull, wielding a sandal, and swinging from the bannister screaming *'I'll never sleep again'*...meanwhile Zachary appears to have eaten several packets of Duracell batteries as he's screaming and jumping around in his chair like a box of ferrets.

I go to find my girlfriend who is huddled under the sink like a ball of wool, whispering to herself and drinking washing up liquid. The house looks as if we've just finished hosting a three day acid party we weren't invited to.

'They're yours for the evening', my girlfriend says. She looks dejected, like she's one tantrum away from fashioning a noose out of a kitchen towel and hanging herself from the ceiling. In my girlfriends mind I haven't been at work all day, I've been sipping cocktails on a yacht somewhere in the Caribbean.

I make a mental note to sign myself up for as much overtime (paid or unpaid) as is legally permissible to do, before walking half asleep into the living room to find Dick and Dom destroying my furniture and making as much noise as their lungs will allow them to.

Shopping

I HAD PUT IT OFF FOR TOO LONG but there was no escaping the inevitable now. Earlier I had opened the cupboards to find half a tin of gherkins, a cucumber that looked older than the birth of modern man and an empty bottle of milk. It was time to do the '*big shop*'. The alternative would mean the kids were going to have to share a plate of gherkins or face the very real possibility of starving to death. Unfortunately my girlfriend wasn't home so it meant braving the shops alone... with two kids.

On a list of things I'd rather not do, you'd find (very high up the list), shopping with kids.

Having found a trolley the size of Bristol to accommodate a three month year old in a car seat, we began our quest.

My daughter has a deep, burning desire to try and get herself lost or kidnapped and within 4 seconds of entering Asda she took off like a cheetah down the fruit isle. I tried to pursue her but the trolley had all the manoeuvrability of a bungalow on a skateboard.

Having caught up to her she was holding a bag of apples and a jar of peanut butter and looking around wildly like a maniac. She then spotted the toy section so before I could tie her to the shopping trolley she darts over like a blow fish and picks up a doll. 'Put that down please!'

'*I want it!*'

'No, you have more dolls at home than I have pence in the bank'…..

What followed was a theatrical spectacle of fireworks, worthy of an Oscar, as she proceeded to throw herself on the floor like a salmon and wail in a pitch that was barely audible to humans.

Being in a Tvery public place with people glaring at me, I had to calmly ask her to stand up, when every fibre of my body wanted to beat her repeatedly round the head with a frozen chicken. Meanwhile I get a strong whiff of something repulsive, I look down to see Zachary's face immediately knowing he's unleashed a poo like an NFL football. This was one of those moments where I genuinely wanted to cry.

Eventually after peeling my daughter up from the floor we carried on (hastily) with the shopping, with my daughter screaming and my son smelling like he'd been left in a tip on a hot day. Of course we still managed to squeeze in another 650 games of *'where in Christ has Phoebe gone?!'* before we'd finished.

I do all my shopping online now.

Third Child

ONE OF MY GIRLFRIEND'S FRIENDS came around with a new born earlier. I was offered the opportunity to have a hold but I was quite content with rocking my 3 MO to sleep whilst he screamed sweet nothings into my ear and begging my daughter to play with *anything* but the 'craft set'.

I looked over as my girlfriend was holding this baby and I thought for a second I caught a glimpse of broodiness from her. After her friend had left I confronted her and told her under no scenario that existed in any universe would there ever be even a part of me that would want to do this a third time.

If she wanted a third child I'd kindly step aside and let her find a new man in her life.

The thought of having another child is, even as I type this, so utterly abhorrent to me that it makes me want to cut off my own jaffers with a pizza cutter.   It's not that I don't love children - which I don't (mine aside) - it's that I'd imagine bringing a third child into our lives would be the equivalent of being set on fire whilst someone was trying to forcibly hand you a baby to hold.

It's just... Too. Damn. Hard.

Boring Labour

LABOUR IS A MAGICAL EXPERIENCE. It's not, it's long and boring and it feels longer than the time it took to create present day Earth.

For hours you're sat there while your girlfriend is in excruciating pain, incapable of conversation and sucking on incredible amounts of Oxygen like a crack addict. You've had no sleep so you're tired and grumpy and it's just so fucking boring.

In the haste to get to the hospital I had forgot to take any form of entertainment apart from an iPad with no Wi-Fi and one game. The game involved a shark you control as you swim slowly around eating small fish. This was mildly entertaining for about 15 seconds after which I wanted to smash the iPad repeatedly against my face until it stopped. But with nothing else to do apart from say *'just breath'*, I carried on playing, swimming slowly and pointlessly around the water as a shark eating fish.

I couldn't tell you what the actual purpose of the game as... or even what it was called, as having left the hospital I threw the iPad under a bus.

The Steriliser

SO WE ARE NOW THE PROUD OWNERS of a steriliser .

It's the size of a Chinese takeaway and the most hideous looking contraption ever designed. We've had to re-organise the kitchen to accommodate it - but it's essential so we'll live with it.

In order to use this thing in the correct manner, you must have the precision and nerve of a brain surgeon.

You have to wash all bottles and teats thoroughly before applying 5ml of water and switching it on. Then after an hour, you must carefully remove each element of the bottle with a sterilised tongue and assemble within the sterilised lid.

Any contact with human skin or any other surface renders the entire process useless. The pressure is in-credible. This is tricky during the day but infinitely more complex at 2am when it's dark and cold and your fucking exhausted.

Trying to feed a teat through a bottle with a small pair of tongues without touching any of the bottle apparatus at 2am makes me look like I'm extracting uranium in my undies.

Following this you take on the role of 'chemist' as you carefully fill each bottle with a specified amount of boiling water. This has to be done every day and is so mind-numbingly tedious I'll purposefully scold myself with boiling water so I feel something other than boredom.

'Google' recommends sterilising bottles until their 12 months old. That basically means I have to repeat this process 365 times.

The day I can get rid of this thing and not have to sterilise bottles is going to be up there with one of the greatest days of my life. I'm going to ceremoniously take it out into garden where I will continue to smash it pieces with a shoe.

Taking Turns Eating

SO TODAY WAS THE FIRST FULL DAY with our new baby on our own, no family or friends or health visitors. Just me, my girlfriend and our daughter. And it was fucking horrible.

My daughter screamed and cried all day, and we sat in the backroom taking it in turns to hold the baby whilst the other one went outside and screamed in the shed.

We're both absolutely exhausted and our lives have been turned upside down and we're both looking at each wondering what the hell we've just done.

I keep trying to start an argument with my girlfriend in the hopes she kicks me out and I can move back home with my Mum for a while.

I made us a lovely meal earlier and we had to eat it in shifts whilst trying to calm an hysterical baby.

Nothing illustrated our new lives more than when, during my turn to have a bit of food, I was slowly cutting up my steak whilst I watched my girlfriend rocking back and forth with a screaming baby with a look of complete and utter resignation on her face.

Imagine trying to enjoy a forkful of potatoes while somebody repeatedly slaps you on the side of the face with a screaming fish - that's what it was like.

What a romantic evening. Baby finally asleep. We're just lay here, holding each other, ears ringing, crying...

The Christening

MY GIRLFRIEND STARTED OFF by saying that my daughters christening should be a low-key affair.

'We'll just book a small local church, and have the post christening gathering at our house, just invite a few close friends and family and keep the cost low.'

After an hour on the iPad she's trying to book St Paul's Cathedral for the weekend. I've never met anyone with such elaborate taste.

She wants my daughter to gallop in on a unicorn dressed head to toe in diamonds and pearls, while a million tender white doves flap elegantly beside her as a hundred thousand Galapagos turtles dressed in velvet hats and carrying single white roses amble slowly beside her singing 'God Save the Queen'.

The christening is then conducted by a group of beautiful mermaids, who start to sing a song so beautifully, that everyone in the room melts into their seats leaving only a pile of clothes. My daughter is then presented with a tiara and named princess of the world.

The Smell (Toilet Talk)

IF YOU POURED A HUNDRED CAT SHITS into a bucket and added mustard, sour milk and dog food, before vacuum sealing the bucket and leaving it to slow cook for 100 days in 104 degree heat the smell created wouldn't even close to the smell of a baby's poo when they have diarrhoea.

It's absolutely revolting.

Earlier I was heaving up my intestines trying to change my sons nappy while simultaneously trying not to choke to death on my own vomit. I've experienced it on both ends of the spectrum. From the super liquid turds that eject faster than the speed of light and have the ability to cover every inch of furniture you love. To the turds so hard and compact you have to perform emergency massages and leg movements to get them out.

I've found the topic of baby shit an increasingly recurring and common topic within my day to day conversations.

This morning I spoke to my girlfriend for 20 mins about the texture, colour and smell of Zachary's latest turd.

'So, was it soft or hard?' 'Yes, but how soft? 'Was he struggling, or did it come out okay?' 'What did it look like? 'Did you taste it?'.

It was only after I got off the phone that I realised that we spend large chunks of our conversations talking of nothing but shit. I can't believe the sheer volume of time and depth of analysis I've taken when discussing my children's shits.

We used to talk about films, holidays, music etc.
They were simpler... shit free... times.

Settling Down

SO, ME AND MY SON have developed this fascinating game of strategy and perseverance.

It takes hours and you're liable to want to ram your face in to the toaster once you've finished - but hear me out. First you get your baby to sleep through rocking and walking for an indeterminable amount of time, but usually about an hour.

Then when your baby is asleep, you have to put them into the cot without them waking up. What's so brilliant about it, is that 97% of the time your baby will immediately wake up and you get to do the whole game over again!

I put him down so delicately that it creates less impact than a single snowflake striking the ground. I then lower myself to floor on my belly and slither out of the room like a serpent so not to be seen.

Typically I make it to the doorway before my son's internal alarm starts ringing and he wakes up as if I've left him in the middle of woods on his own to be raised by a family of aggressive badgers rather than in his warm cot. Me and my girlfriend have been rock, paper and scissoring it for who gets the opportunity to enjoy this game.

My girlfriend spent so long upstairs the other night I'd forgotten she existed. I'm just biding my time for when he's a teenager and enjoys sleep immensely. I'm going to walk in his room and lie on the floor and scream at him but without actually telling him what I want.

Hide And Seek

SO, MY DAUGHTER HAS DISCOVERED the game of Hide and Seek. It's the simplest game ever, but she finds it utterly fascinating and wants to play it all day every day.

I have no problem playing it, but when you've played continuously for 5 hours using only two rooms (living room and dining room) it becomes incredibly tedious.

It's especially tedious as my daughter is unfortunately the worse hider in the universe.

There isn't anyone who's ever played hide and seek in the history of hide and seek who is as monumentally appalling at hiding as she is. She also refuses to let me hide so the game goes like this; I count to ten slowly, whilst my daughter runs into the middle of the room and holds a cushion up to her face. I then have to walk around the room pretending I can't see her before she throws the cushion down and shouts 'here am I'. At which point I act stunned and proclaim her as the best hider ever. She then tells me to count again and she runs in the other run and crouches behind a photo frame.

I'm never allowed to be the one who hides either, which is unfortunate as I'd use the time to hide in the garden and have a nap.

Romantic Nights

FOR THE PAST FEW NIGHTS me and my girlfriend have been sitting downstairs pretending we're still a young couple in love enjoying an adult evening; Watching a film, having a couple of drinks and some light conversation.

But we have kids... so - no.

We have the TV on so low that only an expert in lip reading can understand any of it. We watched a full film last night, entirely in pictures. We don't need sound anyway, we have a built in entertainment centre known as the baby monitor. It sits next to us randomly crackling and hissing like a casserole pot, before spontaneously bubbling out a random shriek like a hysterical witch.

The anxiety of knowing that at any minute a high-pitched scream will come belting out the monitor means it's impossible to relax. So we sit in darkness, looking at a silent TV, whilst simultaneously listening to the monitor and gently trembling and sweating through immense anxiety.

We talk in whispers, which seems senseless as we're downstairs but our children have the hearing capabilities of an African Fruit Bat. Even the food we eat has to be quiet. So we sit in darkness eating soup. We then get to 9pm, congratulate ourselves in silence on our ability to still have a normal life and creep up the stairs like ghosts and get in bed.

Possessed Parents

SPEAKING TO SOMEONE WITH A CHILD is like speaking to someone possessed by Satan.

'Yeah it's fine, I think I'll be heading there on PHOE-BE!! FOR THE LOVE OF GOD PUT THAT DOWN!..Tuesday, I reckon, maybe Wednesday. What do you fancy for tea later STOP BITING THE CAT!, I was thinking chicken and pasta maybe? I'll have to nip out though and pick up some... RIGHT PUT DOWN YOUR BROTHER AND GO AND SIT ON THE NAUGHTY STEP, NOW! Bits first, What time do you think you'll be... WHATS WRONG WITH THIS CHILD, WHY IS SHE EATING COAL FROM THE FIREPLACE! I GIVE UP... heading home?'

That's how 98% of my conversations pan out with my girlfriend these days. We probably speak a couple of times a day. When I'm at work and I ring her I can tell within 0.3 seconds the type of the day she's having by a) the tone of her voice and b) the background noise I can hear. Sometimes she'll answer in a jolly tone and I won't hear anything in the background. This is a good sign. However this phone call happens one in every 11,000 phone calls. More typically she'll answer the phone like a Triceratops that's just been woken up from a long nap and asked to mow the grass. I'll hear what sounds like a cattle market in the background; my son screaming and my daughter demanding cereal.

'How's it going'? I'll ask tentatively before she responds with a tirade of woe. How Zachary hasn't stopped screaming for the past three hours, and won't let her put him down, whilst my daughter has been on a one-man mission to destroy the house.

Nappies

ONE OF MY LOWEST CONCERNS before having a baby was changing a nappy. I had obviously never done it before, but even with my lack of general common sense and inability to perform the simplest tasks I didn't think it beyond the realms of my capabilities. I've since learnt that it's like trying to put a leotard on a cat.

At least on 70 occasions I have managed to get the nappy on the wrong way round and almost always either put the nappy on too tight so the babies legs are at severe risk of falling off. Or so loose that I might as well have stuck them in a pair of adult sweatpants.

Putting a nappy on becomes infinitely more difficult at night when, whilst trying to keep it dark you have to try and move your baby into position and secure a nappy to them. It's like the words shittest game of pin the tail on the donkey.

Invariably at night, after stripping your baby down and realising that they've done a poo the size of a toasted teacake, you realise they have shit welded to their back and legs. You look around and discover you've left the fresh nappy and the baby wipes in the other room. This always happens when your girlfriend has put fresh white bedding on that very evening.

You run in complete darkness to grab the nappy and return to find that your baby has rolled 17 laps around your bed leaving a trail of poo around your bed like a Scalextric track.

Because it's 3am you literally don't care about anything at this point, so after a couple of half-assed dabs you leave the shit on the bed to deal with in the morning. You're literally sleeping in shit and you couldn't care less despite the smell eroding the hairs in your nostrils.

Eventually it does get it easier however. I can safely say I'm now an expert. I could change a baby's nappy with just my feet, whilst blindfolded and riding a wild horse on top of mountain.

So Fat...

'I'M SO FAT'. If I could summarise pregnancy into a short sentence it'd be that.

I have heard those immortal words so often I'm sure it's just become a natural spasm when my girlfriend says them now.

She's not fat, she's just pregnant, as I've tried explaining a million times. But so often I've found her rummaging through her wardrobe, kicking the shit out of a cardigan or a top because it's *'too small'*. It's too small because she's 7 months pregnant and currently has a large medicine ball for a belly.

She has enough clothes in her wardrobe to open an international clothing boutique whilst my wardrobe consists of a small shoe box under the sink. Yet apparently there isn't a single item of clothing she's able to wear. At least 97% of our plans, end up with us not leaving the house because after an hour of battering her wardrobe, finds she only has her PJ bottoms and a woolly hat to wear. She refuses to buy maternity clothes though, so it's inevitable she won't be able to slip into a pair of size 10 jeans without them looking like they've been tattooed on to her legs.

As a kind gesture I thought I'd buy her some maternity clothes myself. I quickly learnt that maternity clothes are just like normal clothes but 700% more expensive and stretchier. They also come in only one of two colours -

black or white. So when we go out now my girlfriend looks like a photo negative of herself.

Working From Home

I WORKED FROM HOME TODAY when my daughter was also home, not something I usually do as it's almost impossible to get any work done.

I'll leave the room to find she has deleted something I've spent all morning completing or she's sent an email to the head of the department which reads sdfkjdfjhiojiijipop[[

Today however I had a pretty important conference call which I was chairing. Deep in conversation about project plans and deadlines etc., with everyone listening intently (well, listening) I was interrupted by a very loud shout from the bathroom. *'DADDD!, I've pooed on the toilet seat!!!'*

It was so loud and disturbing that I literally stopped mid-sentence and completely forgot what I was going to say. Eventually after stuttering for 30 seconds I hung up and raced up stairs. She had indeed pooed on the toilet seat, and the floor and her legs. For someone so small it's quite impressive how big her shits are. This one in total mass was double the size of her torso.

After cleaning her up and bleaching the entire bathroom I finally dialled back into my meeting. I claimed technical difficulties - which was at least partially correct.

Hormones

I'M DONE WITH LIVING WITH A PREGNANT PERSON. It's like living with a hand grenade that's been deep fried in cayenne pepper and then baked in a casserole dish of tears. The hormonal ups and down are killing me.

She cried the other day because we had run out of butter. Absolutely anything can set her off at this point. I left a spoon on the side the other day and I may as well of had an affair with her sister, as she erupted like a volcano of hormones and chucked the spoon at my head and screamed that the house was ALWAYS a fucking mess. Again... there was *ONE* spoon left on the side.

I was listening to her earlier slamming wardrobes and banging drawers upstairs and shouting that she was too fat and she had nothing to wear. I had two choices at this point; I could have leapt through the downstairs window and drove somewhere, or I could try and console her. I made the mistake of choosing the latter.

I crept gingerly into the bedroom to find her having a fist fight with a jumper. *'You look beautiful to me'* I said with doughy eyes….

'Oh piss off Ben, I look hideous and you know it!'

By this point it was safe to say that any further words from me would invoke the full fury of pregnancy, so I just slowly shook my head in disagreement and moonwalked out the door and back downstairs.

Packing For Holiday

YOU'D FORGIVE ME FOR THINKING I was going on holiday with Beyoncé, rather than a two year old.

In order to fit all of her clothes in the suitcase I have to survive the week with one pair of shorts, a vest and a toothbrush. Phoebe meanwhile could change outfits every 7 minutes and still only wear about 3% of what we're taking for her. My daughter honestly couldn't care less what she's wearing and we could have packed her 7 identical potato sacks and she wouldn't have batted an eye-lid.

My girlfriend meanwhile, seems to think that our daughter has to look like she's guest starring in a John Lewis advert at all times.   We're also taking Toys R Us with us as well in case she gets bored. The suitcase weight limit is 22kg; our case weighs 400 metric tons and is the size of Johannesburg.

'Does she really need 11 different straw hats?' I asked as I almost snapped my spinal cord in two trying to force the case shut. The look I received back told me that she definitely did. I didn't bother to ask about why a two year old would possibly need 30 different evening dresses for a 7 day holiday.

Needless to say, it's going to be muggins here carting this monstrosity of a suitcase, containing over 70 pairs of kids sandals half way around the world.

Getting Home

SO WE ARRIVE HOME with our second bundle of joy having had less than 3 hours sleep in three days. I'm ready to gently slip into a 2 month coma and my girlfriend is actually asleep standing up.

My daughter, completely understanding and sensitive to our delicate position asks whether she can get the craft set out, asks whether she can have a packet of crisps and that she needs a big poo.

She wants to do all these three things at the same time. This I know, is just a slither of an insight into life with two kids. I text my Mum and asked whether she would mind babysitting for a 3-4 weeks until we'd caught up on sleep.

The feeling is surreal.

After three years we've finally slipped into a routine and learned how to handle our very demanding three year old. Now there's two of them. My girlfriend goes for a lie down and leaves me with them both and I'm honestly so overwhelmed.

The baby starts crying, then my daughter starts crying because the noise is deafening, then I'm crying because I have absolutely no fucking idea what I'm supposed to do in this situation. I rock the baby whilst trying to console my daughter and telling her everything will be alright.

Like me, she knows I'm lying.

Bribery

SINCE HAVING KIDS my use of bribery has increased about 300%.

There isn't an activity in the world my daughter will do without some form of reward. *'Phoebe for the love of all things holy, if you please eat just 5% of you lunch, you can have this entire chocolate gateau'*....

'Phoebe, if you please let me put your second sock on, you can have a Kinder Egg the size of Sweden'. '

'Phoebe if you brush your teeth you can stay up until midnight and paint the couch in glitter'.

It's become ridiculous.

Also my level of enthusiasm and creativity for the world's most mundane items has increased ten-fold. 'Oh my lord! Look at this magical bowl of princess vegetables!'....'ooOOooh Phoebe! I wish I was allowed to tidy up and get an early night, that's what magical fairies do!' Of course, she rarely buys any of it. She's three years old with the cunning and wisdom of an old Buddhist monk.

'Daddy I'll tidy up if I can have that Lion bar you've hidden extremely poorly in the cupboard'.

I often find myself pleading with her and sounding like a desperate ex lover at times. I'll be outside ASDA giving her a prep talk before we head in.

'PLEASE, Phoebe if you are good in Asda and don't scream because I won't buy you a pineapple or some other

random item you don't really want I promise I will ring Santa and tell him to buy you so many presents it'll take you till Halloween to open them all'....

It usually ends with me carrying her out of Asda 3 minutes later kicking and screaming because I wouldn't buy her an 12 piece dinner set whilst telling her that I'm going to ring Santa and order him to set all her presents on fire.

The Hangover

BEING ABLE TO GO OUT AND SOCIALISE when you have kids requires you to become a project manager, seek planning approval from the local council and requires a 3-4 month lead time for official acceptance.

Having completed the requisite formalities I was free for a night of drinking on the town with no responsibility. Admittedly this feeling of liberty overcame me to the point where I felt the urge to drink excessively. I used to be able to drink heavily and dance until the morning light was appearing and even then was only stopped because of lack of funds.

Last night by about 9pm I wanted to crawl under the table and sleep like a cat in a wicker basket. Incredibly I ended up rolling in about 2am. I used to be able to sleep the hangover day away in bed watching TV and eating my weight in junk food.

That's *before* kids.

My hangover of death kicked in at 6:30am, when I was awoken by the pitter patter of energetic feet. These days it'd take me less time to recover from traumatic surgery than it would to overcome a hangover - I was in no fit state to deal with kids.

I managed to prise my eyes open; it felt like my head had been detached from my body, chucked in the washing machine on high-spin, used as a hammer and then reattached to my torso.

'Can we go to the pumpkin patch today?' my daughter asks.

The mere thought of leaving my bed, apart from to be violently sick, is unfathomable. I looked over at my girlfriend with a pleading look hoping she'd allow to me die peacefully in bed.

Nope.

Fast forward two hours and I'm stood in a field surrounded by bastard pumpkins in the freezing cold. I keep hoping that one of the pumpkins explodes and I'm killed in the blast to end my misery.

I look like a ghost.

I tried to smile a few minutes ago and almost collapsed.

I also feel dirty and highly flammable from the alcohol consumed last night. The next time I want a drink is when I'm offered a small glass of champagne at the christening of my second grandchild.

Swimming

SO I TOOK MY 15 month old daughter to her swim lesson on my own today as my girlfriend was working.

She'd left me with a set of instructions so long and detailed that it left me genuinely petrified.

'Make sure you put on her socks, dress her in the white dress, make sure you put on the green cardigan, make you button up the cardigan, take a box of raisins for a snack but only AFTER she's had her lesson, don't feed her after midnight...' etc. etc. The list went on.

I felt like she had left me alone with a gremlin, that if I didn't follow the instructions to the letter, would start to vibrate like a power drill and reproduce... The swim lesson was fine - I've done that a million times before - the difficulty was in getting us both dressed again.

The women's area to get dressed with their kids is like a big a concert hall - I however had to make do with getting us both ready in what I can only assume is where they keep the spare mop. Phoebe absolutely hates getting dressed/undressed so she started screaming incessantly. Her swim suit, now wet, had welded to her body and looked like somebody had painted it on.

No matter how much I yanked at it wouldn't even move. I feared I would have to call 999 and have her surgically removed out of it. It also didn't help that because she was herself was also wet - she was like a big bar of soap.

Every time I picked her up she'd slip out of my hands like I was holding a seal that'd been covered in baby oil. I rubbed her with a towel to try and dry her to see if that helped but I was rubbing that frantically that I was in danger of setting her on fire. Eventually I got it off. I then realised I'd left the bag of her clothes outside.

I sprinted out to grab it and slipped over, almost cracking my skull in half. I ran back in to find Phoebe had rolled across the changing table and was about to fall off. I grabbed her just in time. It then took me 30 mins to put on the 75 layers of clothes I'd been instructed to put on. Nappy, tights, socks, t-shirt, dress, vest, hat, scarf, top hat, waist-coat etc. When she was finally ready I got myself dressed in under 4 seconds, still dripping wet. The screaming was now so loud I was convinced I had perforated an ear drum. I ran out past the hydro pool and slipped again, this time dropping Phoebe who rolled towards the edge of the pool.

I quickly managed to scramble towards her and grab her. It was the only time I've ever taken her swimming on my own. Since then, if my girlfriend is working I just splash her with a bit of water before she gets home and tell her we had a great time thanks.

Photography

THERE IS NO QUESTION that my son and daughter's lives are the most well documented in history.

My girlfriend takes upwards of 700 photos an hour of both of them.

If you printed all the pictures taken of my daughter over the past three years, you could actually see a minute by minute re-enactment of her entire life. It's a good job neither suffer from epilepsy, as they'd be fitting on the carpet like a couple of carps.

I thought when my son was born, the novelty of would have subsided but if anything it's increased.

When I log on to FB or Instagram, my entire newsfeed is just pictures of my son and daughter dressed in an array of different outfits.

When I'm at work she must spend untold hours changing their outfits and getting them to pose. One minute Zachary is dressed in what I can only assume is cabaret outfit, and then 5 mins later there is another picture of him dressed as an astronaut. Phoebe spends her days wearing elaborate frocks or being made to pose as an fucking shepherd.

My daughter is going to arrive at school on her first day and be bemused as to why no one is taking pictures of her. When we go out as a family, it's like we've got David Bailey tagging along.

Anything warrants a picture being taken.

Unfortunately Phoebe is at an age where she'd literally rather do anything else than pose for a picture. So if we go out we spend 75% of the time trying to bribe my daughter to have her photo taken.

When the 'good camera' comes out it gets ridiculous..

'Ben, get Phoebe to hold that twig, whilst looking mysteriously at the sky'. It'd be easier to get a squirrel to pose whilst doing a cartwheel.

I have to play jester and try and focus all my daughter's attention on taking the perfect picture.

Our photo albums look like the Next Winter/Fall catalogue. We look mysterious and incredibly happy. In reality the picture you're currently looking at has taken 45 mins to set up, and whilst I'm smiling, I've lost all my patience and 4 toes to frost bite, whilst standing in a puddle with my daughter looking like we're spotted something awe-inspiring on the horizon.

Paddling Pool

WHAT HAVE I PURCHASED!? My daughter wanted a paddling pool, and keen to impress her, I bought one from Amazon because the people in picture looked like the happiest anyone has ever been.

She would have been happy with a large bucket of water, but because I'm an utter spaz, I went and purchased a paddling pool of such extravagance that her head would explode with excitement when she saw it.

Well it arrived, and fuck me what have I done!

As usual I didn't once read the reviews/measurements/instructions. It arrived in a pretty biggish box which was fine. When we actually opened it and unravelled it though we discovered that it was in fact, the size of Belgium.

It took about 11 hours to blow it up, by which point I had died (almost) twice from carbon monoxide poisoning. It requires 80% of the worlds available fresh water to fill, and has its own post code. Phoebe will be able to enjoy her 16th birthday in it by the time she's got from one end to the other.

I've got a fairly big garden and this thing covers every blade of grass. It's got slides and tunnels and working sprinklers and inflatable animals. I've just purchased an inflatable circus.

Phoebe was indeed very excited, as she asked me 50,000 times whether she could 'get in yet?' whilst I was blowing this thing up, bright red with a mist descending over my eyes.

To deflate and re-box this thing will require an engineering mind of such brilliance as to baffle the scientific world.

Lesson most certainly learnt.

Constipation

MY SON HAS BEEN CONSTIPATED for a few days now, and he's been proper struggling - bless him. He was pushing that hard earlier that I thought his head was going to pop off like a champagne cork.

No idea why he's constipated. He drinks milk and that's it. Watery milk at that. It should be flying out of him like a jet spray.

But it wasn't...

'Ben, I can see his poo, it's stuck'….I looked - it was indeed stuck. In fact it looked like somehow the poo had taken the form of a large brown Rubix Cube. My poor son was screaming trying to get this thing out of him….my girlfriend looks at me, *'Ben, you'll have to get it out'*….'

'No chance'.

I'm a hands on parent and don't mind changing nappies, but pulling turds out of an arse hole was not in the job description.

The cries of pain grew louder, and my girlfriend got increasingly more panicky, *'Ben it needs to come out now'*… I now felt like a surgeon with a life or death split decision to make. I had to step up.

I made a weird howling noise to try and mask what I was about to do, and then I secured my hands to the end of the dank monstrosity and pulled. It was like pulling a giant turnip out of the soil.

I pulled and pulled and finally it flopped onto the floor like a massive brown haddock.

I felt a weird sense of pride which I imagine is comparable to when a midwife delivers a baby after a traumatic labour.

Ah, memories...

I have since doused my hands in petrol and set them on fire - me and my son have agreed not to make direct eye contact for a few weeks.

I rest a little easier knowing that when I'm much older and incapable of looking after myself I'll have someone to do it for me if the need arises.

The Club

I GET A SICK SENSE OF SATISFACTION when new parents come into work looking like they've spent the night at the bottom of a well.

My body has adjusted to the rigours and brutality of sleep deprivation and I'm a seasoned veteran when it comes to resisting the urge to not want to eat your own face when your child wakes up every 15 mins. I tend to give them the same shite and meaningless platitudes people offered me when I constantly wanted to cry, *'it gets easier'.*

It doesn't really - the difficulty just evolves.

New parents will look you in the eyes like a lost rabbit and ask you questions - desperately seeking reassurance.

A colleague you used to talk about football with is now asking whether it's normal for a baby to scream - high-pitched for 5 solid hours. Another who looked fresh faced and full of beans, now has that perpetual look of sorrow etched on his face - he's now turned the colour of granite.

They've joined *the club.*

It's an exclusive club where conversation is limited to the topic of sleep or baby shit, and where you can only socialise if an event is planned several hundred months in advance. A club where people can see your face actively rust. Membership costs your entire monthly wage and 98% of your free time. When you've joined this club, time takes on a different dimension.

I messaged a friend who I hadn't spoken to in a short while - turned out it'd actually been three and a half years since we had last spoken.

It becomes increasingly difficult to have normal relationships with people not in the club. While their lives are full of ad hoc spontaneous evenings, all you have to offer to the mix is telling your non-member friend that you *only* had to wake up 74 times last night, rather than 84 times. *'I went to the cinema last night and saw a brilliant film'* vs *'you should have seen the size of my lads shit he did at 2am'*.

Shaving

AS WE NEAR THE END OF PREGNANCY my girlfriend is growing increasingly in size and mass.

She's like a giant human beanbag.

I'm convinced this child is going to walk out of her in the hospital and ask for pocket money. Being as rotund as she now is, simple tasks like tying her shoelaces and getting in and out of the car have become monumental undertakings. I try and help out where possible, but last night I think we stepped across the border of what's socially and morally acceptable.

As I was sat watching TV, I was summoned upstairs by my girlfriend who was in the shower. More than a little intrigued I bounded upstairs and into the bathroom. With my birthday over 5 months away I had no idea what she could possible be requesting from me whilst in the shower.

I didn't have to wait long to find out.

'Ben you're going to have to shave me as I can't reach my legs'.

It had clearly taken weeks of building up the courage to actually ask me as her legs by this point looked like they were wearing a Chewbacca fancy dress outfit.

It took me about 2 hours and 7 razors to complete the task. I'd have refused, but I didn't fancy being kicked through the bathroom window by a pregnant girl with carpet legs.

We haven't talked much since the incident.

Working From Home... Again

TODAY WAS A GLORIOUS SUMMER'S DAY and I was working from home.

To take full opportunity of one of only three hot days we get a decade I decided to do my calls in the garden. My daughter was home and was existing happily in the back garden, cycling around on her tricycle, which spends 364 days of the year being smashed to pieces by wind and rain.

In my backyard we have a layer of decking about 3 feet in front of the lawn which is (apart from the steps leading down to it) guarded by rails. My girlfriend was in the kitchen making a drink for Phoebe and I was in the middle of providing an update to a group of colleagues on the phone.

As I'm talking I'm looking proudly at my little girl rolling around on an insanely rusty tricycle, enjoying life and enjoying feeling the sun on her face for the first time in her short little existence.

All of a sudden she turns directly towards the steps of the decking and aggressively picks up speed to about 35mph.

The only time I've seen her move so quickly was when she hears a packet of chocolate biscuits being opened in the kitchen.

The rest happens in slow motion as she rides straight off the decking, over her handle bars, summersaulting onto the concrete path below as her tricycle leaps 20feet into the air before landing on top of her.

My last sentence before I hung up and ran to her aid was *'So as you can see from graph, we've had some very positi…Oh for fucks sake'…*hangs up**

Crawling

AFTER MONTHS OF BEING COMPLETELY STATION-ARY, my daughter is finally crawling. I longed for this day for an eternity. She had mastered the art of rolling on her front, but then would just lay there face planting the floor and getting irritated.

Then she somehow developed the ability to move backwards in a diagonal direction, like a Bishop on a chess-board.

But now she is actually crawling forward. Day one this was an extremely proud moment for me, by day two it had turned me into a neurotic wreck.

She crawls faster than I can run. I put her down and she zips about from room to room to like a hockey puck.

I put her down in the living room yesterday, turned around and she had vanished. I found her several minutes later in the kitchen, trying to crawl through the fridge. The other problem is that I've realised my house is incredibly dangerous and may as well be renamed to the lair knives, fire and torture devices.

Everything poses a threat to a crawling toddler.

They are so incessantly driven to injure themselves it's terrifying. In the space of a particularly challenging 30 minute period; she crawled into the coffee table, tried to eat fire, tried to crawl into the medicine draw and tried to throw herself down the stairs.

Today we've had to go absolutely nuts on the Feng-shui and turn our house in to a featureless barren landscape, void of anything sharp, hard or ingestible.

We've also secured everything we can't move. Our daughter now crawls around in what is essentially a prison cell with a few select (safe) baby toys.

I've become so paranoid that I'm contemplating replacing the laminate flooring with foam.

I think she's deliberately smashing her face on the wooden floor just to torture me.

We now spend our time running around a crawling baby trying to stop it from killing itself. I now miss the times she just lay there.

Hospital Food

WHILST THE HOSPITAL STAFF are generally good, they'd make the poorest hostesses in the world.

I'd been awake for the best part of 48 hours, and my only calorie intake had come from some toothpaste I'd had a couple of days before. I couldn't really leave the room and go and get something to eat or order a takeaway, and being hideously underprepared had bought nothing for us to eat. Not that my girlfriend would have been capable of eating anything.

I was moments away from ordering a Chinese takeaway to the labour ward, when finally one of the nurses offered us some food…. *'do you want some toast?'*….

I could have quite easily married her on the spot.

I was hoping for something slightly more substantial and endearing but at this point I would have gladly eaten the umbilical chord so I happily accepted. 30 minutes later, they popped back in with a slice of bread which looked like it had been de-hydrated, sat on, and then kicked around the maternity ward before used as an ironing board.

I understand the budget challenges in the NHS but didn't realise this extended to the application of butter - I'd never seen a piece of toast so dry. I was scared of touching it in case it started a small fire in the maternity room. With each bite, I thought I was going to choke to death.

They offered me another slice a few hours later, but

I was still chewing the first round of leathery rectangles I'd been given earlier.

It was like chewing on a flip-flop.

Film Time

FILM TIME WITH A THREE YEAR OLD is like watching a movie with the Riddler. It's not the question quality so much that I mind, it's the sheer volume of them, it's unrelenting.

Recently we watched some film about a cartoon Panda, and I may as well have just saved Phoebe the trouble of watching it and just narrated it for her.

'Is it a girl Panda?' What do Pandas eat? Is that one sad? What's he doing with that one? Will there be any baby cats in the film?' This was all before the opening credits had finished.

She doesn't allow you to answer the initial question before starting a brand new question. It's like having a little jack terrier nattering in your ear.

Additionally my daughter's taste in films isn't typical of a normal three year old. Whilst most 3 years olds enjoy Frozen and other Disney classics, Phoebe's favourite film beyond question is... King Kong.

I've seen King fucking Kong 15 million times now to the point it's my least favourite film of all time. It's possibly my least favourite anything.

I know every single line.

It's the longest film ever made, and every time I'm forced to put it on (about 5 times a week) I know I'm in for almost 4 hours of King Kong related questioning.

I know it that well I can tell you the seconds between each people talking. I'd actually venture that I'm the world leading authority on the film King Kong.

Why she's obsessed with it I have no idea.

'Is the gorilla sad?' Why is he angry? Does it like that girl? 'Why is he screaming?'.

Despite me providing these answers *every* single time we've ever watched it, I'm continually bombarded with these same questions every single time.

Grumpy Sleeper

IT'S FRIDAY NIGHT FOLKS - Time to throw on the dancing shoes, hit the bars and paint the town a new shade of red called Ben's sunrise!

In reality me and my girlfriend are prancing around the living room like a couple of jesters trying to entertain a 3 month old who's grumpier than an exhausted fox that's just been woken up by a Jehovah's Witness.

The difficulty in entertaining a toddler who cant speak or move is unrivalled .

I've spent the last 45 hours making silly faces and using my socks as hand puppets and he's not smiled once. I'm starting to irritate myself. Nearly bed time though, when the fun really starts.

Ah Bedtime... when my son gets extremely irritable and pretends he's incredibly tired, but then does a couple of lines of acid on the way up the stairs and becomes more awake than any human as ever been. Then he enjoys being walked around for several million hours on the landing. I walked for that long once that I burned a hole in my slippers. He's not tired, I know he's not but If I have to bring him downstairs and listen to him whinge for another second then I'm afraid I'll snap and throw him through the TV.

So I continue to walk around like a maniac, rocking him and saying 'shhhh' until the noise becomes ingrained in my brain and almost explodes.

When he's finally asleep I put him down and he looks even grumpier when he's asleep.

What the hell has he got to be grumpy about.

I'd love it if someone fed me, changed my arse and rocked me to sleep and tried to entertain me for the entire day the ungrateful little sod.

Restless Night

IN PREPARATION FOR THE INEVITABLE sleepless nights I'll live through when the baby is here, my girlfriend, and deep into pregnancy is giving me a crash course in restless nights.

Her body is going through some truly bizarre behaviour right now. Her body temperature varies between the extremities of hot and cold.

So for part of the night it's like I'm spooning an igloo - then 20 mins later she's hotter than a thermos nuclear reactor, the covers are kicked off, she's thrown all her pillows down the stairs and is sweating profusely.

Her concept of personal space has been abandoned. I woke last night and I was hanging over the edge of my bed unable to move. My girlfriend had spread herself out like a flannel covering 99% of available bed space. She fidgets, moves around all night, constantly itches, frequently hits out and swears.

It's like sleeping with a crack addict.

Fickle Kids

ALL YEAR PHOEBE HAS BEEN OBSESSED with Peppa Pig. It's been the only thing to grace our TV screens from morning till night. Our TV planner is basically just 30 billion recorded episodes of Peppa Pig.

Peppa Pig is basically a cartoon about a know-it-all sow that enjoys jumping in puddles. It's bright, colourful and extremely annoying and I've been forced to watch this fucking pig so much, I feel like I'm one episode away from going and deliberately setting fire to the first pig I see.

But, my daughter loves it. I think it irritates me because everyone in the programme is so stupendously happy all of the time. For 5 solid months she's asked for everything Peppa Pig related. So for Xmas we've spent a small fortune on buying pretty much every piece of Peppa Pig merchandise imaginable; teddies, play sets, stationary, cutlery sets etc. etc. If there is a piece of Peppa Pig merchandise in existence then it's sat wrapped up in the attack. This evening I ask whether she wants me to put Peppa Pig on for her. She looks at me and tells me she *'hates'* Peppa Pig now and that *'its stupid'* . She wants Doc McStuffins on now.

Today is December 23rd. She's got the best part of 40 wrapped presents upstairs, 97% of them are Peppa Pig related. She's going to be incredibly disappointed on Xmas morning unless I can find somewhere willing to swap 150 Peppa Pig toys, for 150 Doc McStuffins toys on Xmas eve.

Using A Spoon

MY DAUGHTERS INDEPENDENCE continues to develop at an alarming rate. She now doesn't allow anyone to feed her, meaning we're forced to sit back and watch her use a spoon like she's wearing large oven mitts. Her coordination is terrible, meaning she piles masses of yoghurt on to her spoon before proceeding to ram it straight at her cheek or forehead.

She had a chocolate yoghurt this evening, and by the time she'd finished it looked as though she'd been replaced with an extremely large Easter egg. She was covered head to toe in thick chocolate, and her high chair had vanished under 4 inches of thick brown goo.

We're going through 15 packs of baby wipes per meal. She must be absolutely starving because I've not once seen her actually guide the spoon anywhere near her mouth. It was very cute at first but having to completely change her and hose down the high-chair after every meal gets tedious very quickly.

We now only allow her to eat in her nappy... in the kitchen... surrounded by discarded newspapers.

On top of being messy - she's an infuriatingly slow eater.

It takes every ounce of patience you can muster to have to sit and watch your child slowly shovel food onto a spoon, before very slowly completely missing her entire mouth and smashing pudding into her eye.

Sleep Routine

WE'VE BEEN TRYING TO get Zachary into a sleep routine as the books recommend; warm bath, quiet, dark room, warm milk etc. We've been doing this at about 7:00pm so he gets used to it being his bedtime, it's absolutely fucking pointless.

The key to making this work relies on our ability to keep the house quiet. The routine has two massive flaws

Firstly, within our house resides a giant 3 year old ball of immense energy that is incapable of sitting still or speaking (shouting) lower than the sound that's created when several hundred cats start mass brawling in the streets.

The *'routine'* subsequently goes a like this; 'Shhh, Shhh' (to Zachary) as we try to calm him to sleep....then *'PHOEBE! For the love of Christ get down of the mantelpiece and stop eating candles!!'* My son is then more awake than he's ever been and the process repeats itself until Phoebe finally blacks out from exhaustion.

The second drawback is that Zachary will only sleep if he knows me and my girlfriend are in the bed next to his cot.

So at 7:30pm on a Saturday night, we're forced to lie in bed, side by side like a couple of fucking corpses, not daring not to move or breathe too loudly. Do you know how difficult it is trying to sleep at 7:30pm on a Saturday in the middle of summer?

It's so bright in my room from sunlight pouring in through the window I've had to apply sun lotion.

You'll be trying to sleep and you'll hear the ice cream van come marauding down your street and hordes of kids, hours away from there own bedtime, screaming with excitement. Meanwhile me and my girlfriend are lay in bed like two gherkins. We can't even talk - he's so sensitive to sound he'll immediately wake up - so we spend our nights communicating through the medium of mime and silent dance.

Lets Eat Out

I USED TO LOVE GOING OUT TO EAT, me and my girl-friend would sit and converse, peruse the menu at leisure and generally enjoy our food and ourselves. Now we have to eat meals with the kids.

We continue to pretend that we're a fully function-ing family unit capable of eating out together, quietly enjoy-ing each others company and having a swell old time.

I absolutely dread the words '*shall we go out for tea tonight*'.

I'm always perplexed when my girlfriend suggests this. It's as if the stress and pain from the previous 35 times we've attempted eating out have been wiped from her memory immediately after having left the restaurant. Like she's forgotten that eating out with a three year old and a 3 month year old is one of the least enjoyable experiences imaginable.

First of all you have to pick a restaurant that's quiet and child friendly, so immediately you know you're going to a restaurant that sells potato smileys with fish fingers and beans.

Then you have to work around nap times/bed times so you end up eating your *evening* meal at about 3pm. You then spend the entire meal begging your daughter to eat just half a fucking carrot, and bribing her with ice cream if she just promises to sit still for more than 30 seconds without sprinting to other peoples tables and creepily staring at them.

Meanwhile the 3MO plays possum, remaining completely still and asleep, until 4 seconds before your plate of food hits the table. Then he's awake and shitting himself - and he's hungry.

So I'll be sat there; feeding a 3MO, screaming at the 3YO to stop putting Bolognese in her apple juice whilst simultaneously trying to cut up my steak using only one hand with a spoon, as my daughter is using the knife to eat her ice cream.

We eat our meals so quickly, just to escape the culinary hell that I find myself with indigestion so intense It feels like someone has poured hydrochloric acid into my stomach.

We have to leave a 150% tip as an apology, as we bundle our shit together and trip over ourselves trying to get out like a group of circus clowns.

Inevitably, we will then get to the car, with my daughter looking like she's dipped her entire head in Ragu sauce and she'll tell us that she's '*lost her shoe*', whilst the 3MO is screaming because he hates his car seat more than anything in the world.

First Night

SO THE FIRST NIGHT WENT LIKE A DREAM. Not an actual dream as you have to sleep in order to dream - which I didn't.

Firstly it appears babies do not like leaving the warmth of their mother's womb for a mosses basket - no matter how prettily it's decorated.

Secondly, they appear to be born equipped as experts in psychological torture.

My daughter spent the entire night (when actually asleep) either breathing so erratically I thought she was doing burpees, or breathing so quietly I kept jumping out of bed and prodding her with a stick to ensure she was still breathing.

In between those exciting episodes were bouts of prolonged crying and feeding. I think I changed her nappy a few times but can't be sure.

However I do smell of wee and have a vague memory to trying to fasten Velcro around a screaming cat in the dark.

Getting To Bed

IT'S SO FUN TRYING TO GET TWO KIDS TO BED.
Forget all this chilling on the couch with a glass of wine
watching mindless nonsense malarkey. Get yourself a three
year old and a 3 month old to jazz up your evenings.

The 3 YO refuses to go to bed until you've read her
at least 7 books, each one of them longer a Stephen King
novel.

The 3 MO won't go to sleep until he's had a gallon
of milk, been walked 17 miles around the house and you're
in his cot, spooning him and whispering nursery rhymes
whilst tickling his earlobe.

I haven't spoken to my girlfriend properly in weeks.
We talk in a series of military commands and signals.

'Ill bath the girl, get her ready; In the meantime, you
flank around the outside and drop the boy 6 ounces of milk
stat. over.

I took the bins out earlier and it was so peaceful and
quiet that I desperately wanted to climb in the green bin to
live out the rest of my life as Stig of the dump.

I actually took them round the block like I was
walking a couple of Labradors to waste time and prolong
the start of the bedtime routine.

Cravings

IN OUR ENTIRE RELATIONSHIP I'd never once heard my girlfriend even mention the word grapefruit, never mind eat one. However for some reason she now eats them by the dozens.

She cuts them in half and douses them in more sugar than is advisable to consume in a decade. She's eating them for breakfast, dinner and tea, and I'm sure I saw her brushing her teeth with one the other night as well.

Invariably I'm the one sent out to get them at any point in the day or night. I was sent out at 10pm recently to Asda to pick up 5 grapefruits, a women's razor and a copy of Heat magazine. I'm pretty sure Asda think I'm on my period, or I'm selling grapefruits on the black market.

I'm spending the equivalent of the total output of a medium sized developed country on grapefruits. We have to keep milk and meats on the decking outside to make room for the bastard things in the fridge. I'm considering bulk buying them from Sicily by the truck load to reduce individual cost per grapefruit.

I tried one out of curiosity, a fruit that's naturally sweet, coated in sugar tastes absolutely revolting. That amount of sugar in one hit plays serious havoc with your mind and body. You can feel your teeth instantly start to rot, and you can feel your heart rate triple and the blood slow down in your veins.

Plus the bitterness of it made my face fold inwards like origami.

Leaving Hospital

'RIGHT YOU CAN GO HOME NOW'... We don't feel ready to be shoved out into the cold, away from the nurses who know what we're doing.

I asked whether it'd be okay if we could stay in hospital for maybe just the first 18-24 months until we're properly adjusted - but nope, we had to leave.

I was terrified... I had images of leaving the hospital and my baby falling down the grid or immediately setting on fire after being exposed to sunlight.

When we got to my car we couldn't work out how the car seat worked and had a blazing row in the hospital car park to the point where I was just going to ditch it and walk the 7 miles home carrying the baby in the car seat like a kettlebell. We had practiced putting the car seat in, but when it came to crunch time it suddenly became comparable to building a rocket capable of orbiting Saturn. Eventually we got it in though, after almost destroying the interior and pulling both hamstrings. The drive to hospital on the way up took about 6 minutes as I was driving like a NASCAR racer.

The drive home with my fragile china pot in the car took the best part of a year. I didn't change from first gear or exceed 3mph. I drove with both hands clamped to the wheels checking all mirrors every 1.5 seconds like a neurotic squirrel.

It probably would have been quicker to crawl home carrying extremely heavy camping equipment, but I wasn't taking any chances.

Playdough

THERE'S A QUESTION MY DAUGHTER ASKS from time to time that makes me turn instantly white.

A question that makes my heart stop and I literally have to sit down before my head implodes... *'Can I get the playdough out?*

I fucking HATE playdough.

It's no exaggeration to say that I'm still finding play-dough in my shoes from when I last allowed her to use it 7 months ago. No matter how much you try and control the playdough activity it ends up absolutely everywhere.

You'll be brushing your teeth in the evening and it find it stuck in the back of your gums. You'll find it hiding it in your Weetabix, or you'll shake someone's hands at work and find playdough on your knuckles.

I've had to lie on a few occasions and tell that the playdough can't be used because it's been stolen by oppor-tunistic badgers. It's horrible stuff and has a number of unique abilities that make it the most irritating substance ever created.

Firstly, It is the only substance I've ever come across with the ability to become as dehydrated as a digestive bis-cuit within 45 seconds of being exposed to Oxygen.. It also acts like an electron within an atom and has the ability to be everywhere and nowhere at the same time.

My daughter will be playing with it in the front

room and I'll open the fridge and it'll be clung to a yoghurt pot, defying laws of physics and common sense.

Labour... Continued

'LABOUR IS A WONDERFUL, SPECIAL EXPERIENCE'. It's not, it's fucking horrible. Seeing your partner writhing in pain, screaming that she' can't do this' and demanding I take her home isn't wonderful. All the while I'm sat there like a spare part saying the words 'just breathe' and 'you're doing so well' repeatedly.

What is wonderful however is when your baby is born, all the relief and emotion just overcomes you. But the moment is marred as the immediate aftermath of birth kicks in.

They thrust the baby in to my arms and sat me down. I looked lovingly into my babies eyes and then, stupidly I looked up. They had seated me directly in front of where the baby had just come out.

Holy shit.

It was like looking at a paper mache octopus. What in the good name of Christ had this baby done down there. It looked like it'd come out wearing a blender for a hat, There was blood and bits of skin everywhere.

I was trying to enjoy the moment with my new baby but I was horrified at what they were doing to my girlfriend. At a time where I was overcome with joy, I was also terrified that my girlfriend now appeared to have grown a tail between her legs.

Labour is undoubtedly the worst experience imaginable. I wanted to apologise to my girlfriend on the behalf of all men for subjecting them to what is effectively torture.

Mornings

THERE IS NOTHING BETTER than having a well de-
served lie in on a Saturday morning after a week in work.
Sleeping soundly and warmly in bed until you lazily open
your eyes at midday. Of course, I wouldn't know anything
about that given my daughter has decided that 5:30am is
now an appropriate time to wake up.

I defy anyone to remain calm when a two YO comes
bouncing in your room at 5:30am like it's Xmas morning.

'Phoebe, please it's early'.

Kids have absolutely no sympathy when it comes to
sleep deprivation.

I let her get in our bed, in the hopes she'd fall back
to sleep, but she was like a hamster trying to put on a pair of
roller skates.

She then started demanding to go downstairs and
watch the fucking TwirlyWoos!. The bastard TwirlyWoos
doesn't even start until 9:00am. After she politely asked me
a further 3 million times, I ripped the covers off and got out
of bed. I stomp downstairs like a petulant child and turn
the TV on.

It's pitch black outside, and still to early for even the
milkman to be out, but there's muggins looking like a ball of
hay in a dressing gown, trying to find the kids programmes.
You know it's early when you're flicking through the TV and
even the children's programmes don't start for another 30

mins, so you and your daughter are on the couch watching a promotional video on an Ab Roller.

I was that annoyed I sat on the opposite couch sulking for two hours trying to explain why we shouldn't wake up when even the owls are still awake.

If you've grown bored of sleeping and fancy having bags under your eyes that you can tickle with your toes then I strongly recommend having kids.

But then she hugged me, and the fact that I've had 4 hours sleep in 8 months seemed irrelevant. I also felt bad that'd I'd be grumpy so I wanted to buy her a pony. She's manipulative like that and has me acting like I'm going through the menopause.

Tired

ON A SCALE OF 1-10, with 10 being the most tired anyone has ever been since the creation of the universe, I'm currently 47.

At about 4am this morning, I went downstairs to make a bottle of milk and came upstairs with a glass of Vimto. My eyes feel like someone has taken them from my head and simmered them on a low heat.

At 3am this morning I was googling how much it'd be to hire a night nurse as I can't cope. I'm generally not too bad with operating on limited sleep, but Zachary only sleeps in 50 mins bursts, and the pressure to force myself to sleep before he wakes up again is immense.

When he finally sleeps you have to try and knock yourself unconscious as quickly as possible.

Despite being insanely tired, and despite the fact your brain has been unable to process a single meaningful thought all day, your brain suddenly becomes Aristotle and wants to decipher the deep questions of the universe at just the moment you desperately need to shut off - *'Whoooahhh there Ben lad slow down, before you dash off to sleep there has you ever considered how truly enormous the universe is?'* - I feel like I've taken sleep for granted.

If I could go back pre-kids, I'd go to bed at 5pm every night and sleep until 2pm the next day, and then have a nap an hour later.

I've also discovered since having kids that I need 5 books, 3 glasses of water and 28 pillow flips before I can sleep. Me and my girlfriend were chatting earlier and got on to the subject of magical powers. *'If you had magic powers what would you do?'* The best we could come up with was the ability to stop time, so we could get a full 8 hours sleep.

That's a true sign that you're older than the mountains and have kids.

Pathetic really.

Clothes

MY GIRLFRIEND PICKS THE CHILDREN'S CLOTHES. I have little to no input apart from providing financial assistance. My daughter has a wardrobe stuffed full of dresses and ball gowns. They are lovely granted, but when you're popping to Frankie and Bennies for dinner and your daughter turns up like she's arrived by magical pumpkin it looks odd, especially when her Dad looks like he's made his clothes himself from an old bath towel.

She does have regular clothes but she's become so accustomed to looking like something from a Disney film she flat out refuses anything else. I've had to take her to nursery before now in the height of winter wearing a frock that had the circumference of a fishing umbrella and made moving pretty much impossible.

My son doesn't faire any better. I was hoping with a boy, I'd be able to have a little more input and the clothes would be a tad more subtle. I came home yesterday to find him dressed up like a yeti, looking like he was about to make his final ascent up Everest.

The other day he was dressed as a gay pirate (I think). I've also seen him dressed as a lion, Indiana jones and a sailor.

The worst are the hats.

I don't know when she purchased them or whether they've been breeding in the draw but my son at 2 MO appears to have acquired the largest hat collection in Europe.

He fucking hates wearing hats, regardless of how many time my girlfriend wings one on him. They also make him like an irritable cabbage patch kid.

The Plane

IT'S ALMOST AS IF PLANES were not ergonomically designed to change nappies mid flight.

My son decided to skip his traditional morning poo and opt to do one over International waters at 10,000 feet.

I'd have left it until we landed but we were about 8 minutes into a 3 hour flight and it smelt so bad the chair fabric was starting to wrinkle like cellophane under a flame.

I grabbed a nappy and wipes and staggered down the aisle to the toilets. I say toilets, it's essentially a phone box with a hole and a tap. The flight attendant kindly showed me that there was indeed a baby changing shelf which she pulled down.

Unless I was changing a gerbil there was no way on this planet a baby would fit comfortable on this changing table. I had to prop him on the shelf at a 45 degree angle, partly on his side with his head wedged against the wall to get him on.

Luckily my girlfriend had put on the worlds most difficult baby grow to undo which made it so quick and easy to get him undressed, on a bumpy flight, in a phone box in near darkness whilst he screamed incessantly at me. This baby grow had about 45,000 buttons, 150 zips and large padlock. It needed a crack team of contortionists to help me get it off.

Eventually I did, only to discover that he had shit

all over his back and legs so had to hold him with one hand to stop him falling 4feet to his death while cleaning up poo with my one free hand. I smashed my head against the top of the sink about 40 times and pulled a hamstring trying to get a new nappy on him.

I finally emerged about 35 minutes with cramp in my arms and legs and my son in just a vest and nappy that looked like it had been put on by an octopus wearing boxing gloves.

Your Turn

I DO IN THE REGION OF 95-99% of all night time feeds. Not because I'm a hero, but because my girlfriend slips into a sleep so deep that doctors would probably pronounce her dead if they checked her pulse.

I sleep so lightly on the other hand that I can hear my sons thoughts while he sleeps. So when I hear him stir, I pounce out of bed like a leopard and leg it downstairs to make a bottle before he properly wakes up and screams the house down and wakes the entire street.

Sometimes when it's my turn, I'll be sat feeding our son at the end of the bed in complete darkness with my retinas on fire due to sleep deprivation and I'll see my girlfriend fast sleep and just... hate her so much. She looks so smug lay there in the warmth.

Occasionally she'll stir long enough to give me a piece of irritatingly obvious advice like '*make sure you put a bib on him*', like she suspects that while she's not watching I'll pour milk directly down his t-shirt so he freezes to death in the night.

When it is my girlfriends '*turn*' to do the feed, I have to basically elbow drop her on the face, and say her name over and over again like I'm summoning the fucking Candyman. By the time she's actually awake my son is so alert that he's doing summersaults in his cot. I'm then also awake as I've had to try and wake up my comatose girlfriend.

She'll proceed to plod downstairs and take an eternity to make some milk.

It'd be quicker if my son clambered out of his cot himself and nipped down to Morrison's and get his own. So whilst she's downstairs making a bottle of milk as slowly as she possibly can, I have to close my eyes and attempt go back to sleep whilst the one man band is in his cot sounding like he's welding a ship.

It's genuinely just easier to get up and do it myself.

Walking

MY DAUGHTER HAS FINALLY STARTED WALKING. I'm very happy as I thought this day would never come. I had images of her crawling to university, and me crawling down the isle with her on her wedding day.

I say walking in the loosest sense of the term, as she actually walks like an old drunk wearing ice skates walking through a field of a peanut butter crunchy. It's also increased her risk of accident by 10,000%.

She's fallen over and cried and banged into something about 60 times already today - its 8:30am. Being a typically independent little girl, she now doesn't want to be carried or go in the pram at all.

We went for a lovely walk yesterday around a big lake that typically takes an hour to walk around. We managed it in no less than 5, by which point it was getting dark.

I spent the entire walk having panic attacks, standing 4cm behind her with my arms open the entire time, and constantly grappling her away from the edge of lake where I'm convinced she was going to jump in head first. At one point I picked her up and she screamed so loudly that people were looking at me like I was about to kidnap her.

I love that she's independent and learning on her own but Christ it's frustrating. We've had to erect dozens of child gates around the house. I'm now like a sheepdog, guiding my daughter through a gate before quickly closing it behind her.

It doesn't help that she can only walk in diagonal lines. Play time is now like baby sitting a pumped up Zippy and Bungle.

Lazy Sunday

'*LETS HAVE A CHILL OUT DAY TODAY*' my girlfriend says one miserable Sunday morning.

I like chill out days, but not when you have kids. Because they don't exist.

Our day pretty much went exactly how I imagined it'd go; 340 snack times by 11am, with me trying to rationalise why you can't have a Fruit Pastel lolly for breakfast, the opening 6 minutes of 77 different films until my daughter was immediately bored and wanted something else on, and felt tips with no lids on scattered across the living room in their millions like fallen soldiers.

I blinked at one point and when I opened my eyes, Phoebe was trying to trace her hand on the couch with black marker.

My son meanwhile had himself a little competition to see how long he could whinge for without his Dad beating himself up with the TV remote.

Time starts defying the laws of the universe and moving so slowly you feel like you're trapped in a alternate reality.

Seconds were like minutes, minutes like hours. Me and my girlfriend have been taking it in turns to go and have naps. If I have to sit and watch another second of children's TV I'm liable to smash my face against the TV screen until I black out and die.

We've resorted to putting the clocks forward 3 hours and pretending it's bedtime.

We're now sat here in a house that looks like we've hosted a the black Friday sales.

Chill out days don't exist.

Hospital Visits

GOING TO THE HOSPITAL FOR SCANS is both exciting and exacerbating.

It's exciting as you get the chance to see your boy/girl on the screen and hear the heartbeat etc. However it's equally infuriating as hospitals are inefficient and are run by a cluster of moronic hedgehogs with not a GCSE between them.

They ALWAYS ask you to arrive at 9am on a Wednesday; peak rush-hour. So you have to set off at 4am to ensure to ensure you have plenty of time to get there without being stuck in miles of traffic.

When you finally get there you discover that everyone has seemingly bought 11 cars with them.

After circling for an hour and realising the hospital underestimated how many parking spots they'd need by 10,000%, you're forced to park illegally - half on a curb and half in a bush - only to then find you've not got £78 in change for an hour parking and you're closer to home than you are to the hospital.

You then discover that hospital directions have been written by somebody with only a cursory grasp of the English language, who is also blind, with no sense of direction and a hatred for everyone.

Before you know it, you've walked about 13km around the hospital and find yourself in the hospital canteen about 45miles from the maternity ward.

When you finally do get there, breathless with only seconds to spare they kindly direct you to have a seat.

The brilliance of hospitals is their ability to give you an appointment time which has a probability of minus 75 of being accurate.

I'd much rather them tell me just to pop in some-time after 9ish. Make sure you always pick a comfy seat, as you'll be there a long time. I waited for so long once I had grown a beard by the time we were seen.

Naps

MY DAUGHTER HAS NOW DECIDED that the only way she'll ever nap again is if I put her in her pram wrapped up like a burrito and walk her around the block at least four times.

I've tried literally everything else beside actually knocking her out.

So come rain, sleet, hail and snow you can find me walking aimlessly and dejectedly around the block with a pram, exhausted and at severe risk of chucking myself under the tyres of a passing car. She'll happily sleep when I'm pushing. If I carried on walking until she was 11 she'd probably stay asleep.

The second I get back home and open the front door she's awake. The alternative is not letting her nap, which means she'll be so irritable and cranky that she'll whinge all day which is a fate worse than death. I'd rather be locked in the bathroom with 3 extremely large and angry crocodiles armed only with a toothbrush than have to listen to a crying baby all day.

When she's older I'm going to come in her room while she sleeps, lie on her carpet and just start screaming. She'll then have to figure out what's wrong with me without me talking and try and get me to settle down.

Hungry Baby

MY SON HAS PUT ON 12 OUNCES IN A WEEK and I'm getting concerned. He must be going through a growth spurt. He's been feeding continually for about 11 hours now like he's at an all you can drink milk buffet. I know it might be a tad early given he's only five weeks old but I'm considering weaning him and going making him a ham and cheese toastie to suppress his appetite.

I caught him earlier on Just Eat, trying to order himself a large donna naan with cheesy garlic pizza and chips - he's an animal. At this rate I'll be getting him fitted for a suit next week. I'm worried ill wake up and he'll have borrowed my car to nip to the shops to buy himself a bag of monster munch and a Yorkie.

If this weight gain continues at its current pace he'll weigh as much as a Fiat Punto by the time he's 6 months. He's ripping through his baby grows like the hulk.

Irritatingly 97% of the clothes he has are new born clothes, meaning he's got 14,000 baby grows which we can only use as a bib. We're going to start having to dress him up in a pillow case. The difference a week or so makes is incredible. I've seen pictures from when he was two weeks old, and it looks like I'm holding a normal two week old baby.

Today I saw a picture of me holding what looks like a very large armadillo in a baby grow.

Overdressed

SO MY DAUGHTER TELLS ME its fancy dress at nursery on Friday. It's Thursday evening. I vaguely remember them telling me something about it a week or so ago but as I have a 5 week old baby, and my brain is sleep deprived and doesn't function.

Not wanting my daughter to be the only one without a costume I rummage through her cupboards and by a stroke of pure magic, find a princess ball gown with tiara we purchased unnecessarily a few months ago.

Perfect.

The next morning I get her ready and find the dress is pretty ridiculous. It has a wingspan of about 11 feet and is so frilly and over the top she looks utterly ridiculous. She looks like a giant pink albatross. I offer to try and find something else but she loves it, despite her inability to move or breath properly in it. It's that big I have to shoehorn her in to car.

We arrive at nursery and I get to her classroom and glance inside - my heart stops.

NOBODY ELSE is dressed up.

They're all wearing casual clothes. It's too late to go back now, so we walk in.

Everybody looks over at my poor daughter who looks like she's arrived by horse and carriage in a Disney film. I'm informed that fancy dress is next Friday and I leave, heartbroken, watching my daughter's nursery friends come up to her and quiz her about why she's dressed like a large wedding cake.

I'm a shit Dad sometimes.

Spider

I'M STILL SHAKING. I heard a loud scream coming from my daughters bedroom earlier, and I bolted up the stairs so quickly I'm throwing in a whiplash claim in tomorrow as I think I've detached my spinal cord.

I burst open the door and my daughter is screaming and pointing at the wall. I turn around and there is a spider the size of a dinner plate clung there like a large photo frame.

This thing was fucking massive.

It had tattoos and was smoking a cigar. I've genuinely never a spider as big and ugly in my life.

If my daughter was expecting her Dad to be a hero in this instance, she was spectacularly disappointed.

I too screamed, before taking off my shoe and throwing it at the spider. It bounced off him like he was on steroids and had spent his entire life doing nothing but lifting weights. It then dropped onto the floor and ran across the carpet like a cat before vanishing into a pile of clothes. After jumping on the pile of clothes for 10 minutes and beating the washing mound with my spider killing shoe, I very tentatively removed the clothes one by one to find what was left of Phil Mitchell the spider.

It was nowhere to be seen - it had vanished.

He's probably nipped down to Weatherspoon's for a curry and a few pints, and he'll come home later tonight, steaming and start smacking me around the house.

I've had to lie to my daughter and tell her I've got rid of the spider. I couldn't possibly tell her that tonight she's sharing her room with a spider the size of an albatross, that's ready for darkness to descend so it can crawl out and possibly eat her whole.

She'd never sleep again... Like I won't.

The Possessed Child

HAVING A THREE YEAR old is like living with a small psychiatric patient, at times it's frightening.

Yesterday she was sat silently watching videos on her iPad, when all of a sudden she looks up and says, *'All lambs are born now aren't they'?...*

I look at her, and she's staring intently at me expecting an answer.

'Erm yeah, they are all born now sweetie'...

She looks at me emotionless for about 45 seconds before going back to her iPad.

The fuck is she watching?

The other night I walked past her bedroom at 10pm and heard her softly singing to herself, a song I'd never heard about a clown. I went into her bedroom and she was lay in bed with the nightlight on just staring into space singing. I've got Goosebumps at this point and ask if she's okay.

She doesn't say anything, she just closes her eyes and goes back to sleep.

Honestly, hands down, the creepiest thing I'd ever seen. I felt like torching the house to the ground to rid the child of evil spirits.

Sometimes, in the middle of the night her bedroom door creaks open... I'll look down the hall to see a small silhouette at the end of the corridor....then she bolts towards my bed and whispers *'I want some milk'...* cue me - part screaming and part agreeing. There isn't a horror film ever created that is 1 millionth as scary as living with a toddler.

Countless Nights

I'VE LOST COUNT OF THE AMOUNT OF TIMES my son was up during the night.

I *think* it was about 176 - maybe slightly more. Then after 11 minutes sleep my alarm went off.

I'm an absolute zombie this morning. It took me a lifetime to get ready for work.

At one point I found myself in the kitchen, just stood there staring at the microwave. I look like I've been at a 24 hour acid rave, ingested 14 litres of Polonium, before blacking out in swamp.

Now I'm going to drive the 40 mile journey to work with all he windows and doors open in the hope I don't inadvertently drive myself off the motorway bridge…. Luckily it's Tuesday… Just 4 days till the weekend… Jesus wept.

It wasn't even that he wanted anything when he woke up. He didn't want feeding or need his nappy changing. I just think he genuinely wanted to test how quickly I'd get to him after the 47th time.

He smiled at me every time I got there, which was cute the first 7 or 8 times, but after the 15th time and knowing I had 4 hours before my alarm went off it, it ceased in hilarity and I wanted to stick in him under the sink.

When I arrived at work, people could see I'd had a rough night.

It was impossible not to as I looked like an extra

from Men in Black.

'It'll get easier' one of my colleagues said.

I had to walk off and go and sit in the bathroom for 10 minutes because that piece of completely and utterly pointless fucking advice was not what I needed right now. I was afraid that in my weary state, if I hadn't have walked off immediately, I would beaten my co-worker to death with my keyboard.

The Shits

I TOOK THE KIDS DOWNSTAIRS this morning to allow my girlfriend a few extra hours in bed. Phoebe was sat watching cartoons as I was changing the little man on the couch - at 6:15am....Half asleep I forgot a) a spare nappy or b) wipes.

So I take his nappy off and he looks at me and smiles. Then he clenches... and literally shits all over my hand, the couch, the floor and his baby grow. I screamed at Phoebe to go get me the baby wipes....she runs in the back room and then doesn't return.

I shouted again.

About 2 minutes later she comes back in... with just ONE baby wipe! By this point, the couch is pretty much ruined and needs incinerating.

'Where are the rest of the baby wipes Phoebe!?' I scream.

'Don't know' she says, nonchalantly as she sits back on the couch and turns her iPad on.

I quickly run in the back room to find the rest of the wipes. She'd hidden them under the table. I run back to find him peeing like a fountain all over the living room.

The smell was revolting, but I pushed forward retching and wiping. I rolled him over to find he even had poo in his hair. I gotten through 11 million baby wipes and 15 tea towels.

But the shit was winning.

I needed help - '*Help me! He's shit on the couch!*' My girlfriend came down as I was sat in the corner of the room surrounded by a billion baby wipes and shit stains on my hands - with shit scattered all over the upholstery like a dank turd inspired monet.

Aaaand....

Breathe....

Epilogue

HAVING KIDS HAS COMPLETELY CHANGED MY WORLD. This sounds an obvious thing to say, and it is, but it's true.

Your life is no longer really your own and everything you did so casually when you don't have kids becomes exponentially more difficult when you do.

Despite some of the horror stories you've just read, and my repetitive tone of sourness, anger and despair I can honestly say that I wouldn't change any of it for the world. The rare occasion when my girlfriend and I don't have the kids with us - we genuinely have no idea what to do with ourselves.

It's too quiet, too normal - no one attempting to do something stupendously dangerous - It's not long before we seriously miss the children.

This lasts about 35 seconds until they've been returned to us and we remember how hair tearingly chaotic and exasperating they are.

I love my children more than I ever thought it possible to love anything or anyone, but on a scale of 1-10 in terms of likeliness of having any more - with 0 being never and 10 being definitely - I'd say I'm currently at minus 11,042.

Never again.

If I thought I could survive without it, I'd have my

penis chopped off immediately.

It's so hard and exhausting - but it is worth it, honestly.

You'll have picked up on the contradiction in my emotions of Dadhood -being at the end of my tether and being in love. That's pretty much the range of feelings you experience on an hour by hour basis as a parent.

This book was never intended to be a book. It was a series of general ramblings I started to share on my social media.

It's not a book on how to be a good parent, it could never be, as I'm still struggling with how to be a parent myself.

Every day presents a new challenge - or a new 'phase'. You can read every parenting book in the world or spend hours googling how to settle a fussy baby or deal with sleep deprivation and it can never truly prepare you for the actual reality of having kids.

It will make you cry, feel exhausted, angry but ultimately it will also make you feel happy and proud. That I can promise.

My daughter is almost 4 now, and my son is 6 months old. Without being too cliché -, time really does go so fast. It felt like only a week ago my daughter was born, a day since she started walking, and about 10 mins since my son entered this world.

My daughter now talks back to me and my son is learning how to crawl and move independently. I'm so incredibly proud of both of them and there isn't a thing in this world I wouldn't do for them.

I know It won't be long until I'm writing about my experiences about kids when they're at school, and when they're both teenagers and then one day... they'll move out and have families of their own and the house will be ours again.

Quiet, tidy, and full of memories, laughter and (plenty of) tears. They'll one day they bring their own children round and complain; that they haven't slept in days, the kids won't eat, and that one of them has set their pet dog on fire.

At this point, I will smile, offer my own useless advice and whisper 'pay back' under my breath.

And maybe let them read this book.